LOVE YOUR LINKEDIN PROFILE

How to build a kick-ass profile, elevate your brand, and get results

Natalie A Berthe, MBA, MA

Sacred Revolution Press

Love Your LinkedIn Profile: How to build a kick-ass profile, elevate your brand, and get results
Author: Natalie A. Berthe

Published by Sacred Revolution Press, Washington DC, USA

loveyourlinkedinprofile.com

Contact publisher for bulk orders and permission requests.

First edition © 2025 Natalie A. Berthe

Cover design by Natalie A. Berthe
Cover formatting and page design & formatting by Leesa Ellis of 3 ferns » **3ferns.com**

Printed in the United States of America.

Library of Congress Cataloging-in-Publication Data available on file.
Library of Congress Control Number: 2025914952

ISBN (Paperback): 979-8-9987998-1-5
ISBN (Hardcover): 979-8-9987998-2-2
ISBN (e-Book):   979-8-9987998-0-8

CONTENTS

CHAPTER 1

LinkedIn: Not Your Average Social Media Platform

WHEN LINKEDIN WAS FOUNDED BACK IN 2002, MySpace, Facebook, Reddit, Twitter, had not yet launched, Yahoo was still king of the search engine, and Gmail didn't exist. Today's average LinkedIn user couldn't yet read, and most of us depended on the free AOL CDs we got in the mail to keep us connected to the Internet. That dial-up tone is still one we recognize today. The Dark Web was still new—just two years old—and Instant Messaging (IM) was the "It Girl" of communication.

It was also immediately after the dot com bubble burst. People were worried about their careers and uncertain about the future, and most of us still had dial-up internet. By all accounts, LinkedIn is *the* dinosaur of social media platforms, outlasting Friendster, MySpace, Vine, and countless others.

So it says something about LinkedIn's staying power that it not only continues to be an active platform, but that its user base continues to grow and its relevance continues to expand.

THE EVOLUTION OF LINKEDIN

According to LinkedIn's website, its purpose is "to connect the world's professionals to make them productive and successful." When it launched, LinkedIn was in practice an open online resume platform that allowed users to connect and look for their next job opportunity. And that's exactly how most people treated it: like another place to share resumes, connect with our coworkers, and not much else.

LinkedIn has evolved considerably since then, especially when it comes to expanding our personal networks of folks who have shared interests, industries, and connections. However, it is, at its essence, still a place to share our work history.

I recently watched a TikTok video by a creator who is leaving the military. She asked her audience what they did, since she was trying to decide her next steps. What I found fascinating was not the number of people who shared ideas, but how often someone else would ask for the commenter's LinkedIn profile so that they could see the path of how that commenter got to where they are currently working. LinkedIn does a really great job of tracking that progression as well as the skills we've acquired along the way.

However, taking advantage of all that LinkedIn offers is not so simple for founders and business owners who aren't playing the traditional employment game. The platform's DNA was built for job-seekers, not deal-makers, founders, or business owners. That's something we need to adapt to work for anybody who uses LinkedIn.

Frankly, how *everyone* uses LinkedIn needs a major overhaul. In a sea of over one billion users, you're going to need more than a basic resume, an uninspired headline, and a boring (or nonexistent) banner to stand out.

EVERYONE USES LINKEDIN

The weirdest part of LinkedIn is that it's the one social media platform that feels required, whether you are a professional, employed by other people, an entrepreneur, an executive, an artist, or a freelancer. No matter the situation—online or in person—someone will inevitably ask you if you have LinkedIn (of course you do!) and will check out your profile. Even if they *don't* ask, they will still look for you on LinkedIn and view your profile.

This isn't true of Facebook, Instagram, TikTok, YouTube, Pinterest, BlueSky, or any other social media platform. No one is going to look at you weirdly if you admit that you never understood Instagram and don't post much over there, or if you don't have a TikTok account, or that you left Twitter/X years ago. Meanwhile, you can't even apply for a job, solicit funding, or launch a business without having a LinkedIn profile.

Ironically, LinkedIn is also probably the least understood of any of these platforms, and the most poorly exploited. You can see it in how bad profiles are and how uninspiring posts can be. The problem is that even though the internet is flooded with LinkedIn profile tips, most focus on surface-level optimization and lead generation (getting leads).

To properly and effectively use LinkedIn, it's important to start with the basics, and that's understanding LinkedIn on a fundamental level.

THE PROFESSIONAL CONVERSATION SPACE

The best way to think about LinkedIn is as an ongoing conversation. Everything about LinkedIn reinforces this idea.

LinkedIn's algorithm is beautifully simple: show up authentically, engage meaningfully, and watch your visibility multiply.

Engagement takes on many forms on LinkedIn. You can add insight to others' posts that you repost, or spark conversations in the comments, or share valuable content with your own perspective. Each genuine interaction expands your reach.

LinkedIn loves a good storyteller and is not so forgiving of a one-way flow of information. Posting infrequently, not participating in the comments, or only sharing announcements about offers or accomplishments results in very little engagement on posts and profiles. And as in any conversation, bragging will only take you so far.

You are invited to participate in whatever way makes the most sense for you, but interactively engaging with others is key.

Unlike other platforms that often penalize viral success, LinkedIn rewards it—the more your content resonates, the more the platform amplifies your voice. The more your voice is amplified, the more people check out your profile, which leads to more meaningful engagement.

In other words, conversations will encourage others to check you out, but it's your profile that will keep them coming back.

NO, LINKEDIN IS NOT AN EXTENSION OF YOUR WEBSITE

A marketing professional once told me that they thought that a LinkedIn profile is like a website, or at least an extension of their website. They aren't alone in this assumption, which is obvious when you see the profiles of many marketing professionals.

In fact, LinkedIn is *not* an extension of your website and should not be treated as such. This is why you need a different strategy than you might use for your actual website. That's not to say that you won't use overlapping elements and language, but success on LinkedIn requires an alternative approach.

The key difference between LinkedIn and your website is how you interact with your prospective clients and network. Your website is a sales pitch about your business and services. People visit your website to learn about your company and expect to be "sold to" or informed to some extent.

Your LinkedIn profile, on the other hand, is about YOU. When someone is checking out your profile, they want to get to know you personally, learn what you bring to the table, and understand what makes you interesting. It helps build the know-like-trust factor that is so important in professional relationships, whether you're looking for clients, looking for a job, or want to expand your professional reach.

This is another reason why it's helpful to think of your LinkedIn experience as an ongoing conversation. When you have a conversation with a real human being, either in person or virtually, you get to know the people involved in that conversation, not only their business or what they do.

WHAT TO EXPECT IN THIS BOOK

If you picked up this book, your LinkedIn profile probably isn't what you want it to be or isn't doing what you want it to do.

You shouldn't feel badly about this. No one has taught us, especially as founders and business owners, the best way to utilize our LinkedIn profiles. Until fairly recently, LinkedIn wasn't designed for us to highlight our businesses and expertise, except on company pages. Plus that LinkedIn-as-resume mentality has been a very hard habit to break.

If you're a career professional or job seeker, you're likely no less confused about the best way to make your profile work for you. After all, what's the point of LinkedIn if all you're doing is repeating what's already on your resume or posted on Indeed?

The good news is that once you define your goal and figure out your messaging, the hardest part will be what *not* to include.

I recommend reading the first few chapters in sequence until you get to *How to Use This Book.* Do not skip the chapter called *Strategy,* since that outlines the crux of what you need to know, which is important as you approach each section. After that, pick-and-choose the chapters relevant to you.

Good luck. I can't wait to hear how your new-and-improved LinkedIn profile works for you!

CHAPTER 2

Looking For A Solution

MY DECISION TO WRITE THIS BOOK is the result of not being able to find a LinkedIn specialist or book to help me figure out how to best create my LinkedIn profile. I wanted to be told how to approach each section, what to include, what to say, and how to say it.

Is that unreasonable? Apparently so. I had no idea just how hard it would be to find someone who really understood LinkedIn and the best way for folks like me—entrepreneurs, founders, business owners—to leverage it. I later learned that this problem is universal to all LinkedIn users, but what is there is definitely geared toward job seekers.

THE LINKEDIN EXPERTS

The first time I went looking for someone to help me fix my LinkedIn profile, I found two people who claimed the title of "LinkedIn expert." The first expert used her About section as a copy of her resume (it literally looked like a resume), which was repeated word for word in her Experience section. I didn't know much about LinkedIn, but pasting resume language into multiple sections? Was that really the best we could do?

Thank you, *NEXT!*

The second expert used her About section to explain in vivid detail the abuse she experienced at the hands of her father. I had no idea what that had to do with being a LinkedIn expert, but even I knew that trauma dump was completely out of place. This is even truer when you consider that this was back when LinkedIn was more formal than it is now.

Needless to say, I didn't hire either one of them.

Over the years, as other LinkedIn experts showed up in my feed, I'd check out their profiles and what they offered. It was always underwhelming.

Most helped folks craft their profile to find a job, which wasn't relevant to me.

Of the "experts" who were business-oriented, most of them focused on what's called "lead gen," or lead generation. They teach people how to generate leads on LinkedIn, often by sending tons of DMs to your "ideal clients." (If you own a business and are on LinkedIn, you've probably received a slew of these messages.) Their profiles were often ugly and hard to read. (Why do they all use red, black, and white as their branding colors? Why are their banners so hard to read? Why do they seem so angry?)

Finally, of the "experts" who focused on profiles of business owners like mine, I noticed that they might do a good job on parts of the profile, but then were missing important information. For example, they didn't have a company page for their business, or they didn't offer a description of what their businesses do. If you're going to hang your shingle out as a LinkedIn expert for business owners, shouldn't you be using, I dunno, the company pages??

Heavy sigh.

Marketers of any variation, from social media managers to branding strategists to chief marketing officers, were rarely any better. And the ones that did it well weren't taking on clients who only wanted help with their LinkedIn profiles. It was like looking for a needle in the haystack to find one that was using LinkedIn in a way that made sense to me and that would work for me.

This is not meant to throw shade on anyone who has tried to improve LinkedIn profiles. Several do parts of their profile well. Many developed techniques that seem to work for them and some of their clients, especially if they niche down to a particular market. And frankly, we need *more* people who know how to do this well, not fewer, because it makes networking on LinkedIn a whole lot easier when we understand who someone is by checking out their profile.

Unfortunately, though, what I'd learned from them didn't work for me, my market, or my clients. So I set out to figure it out myself.

I know people who've spent a lot of money hiring someone to design their profiles, only to be hugely disappointed with the results. I know people who were thrilled that they had someone to hire because they didn't want anything to do with setting up their own profile, simply so they had a presence, albeit an underwhelming one, on LinkedIn.

I didn't want to settle for mediocre or something that didn't work for me. And since you're reading this book, I assume you feel the same way.

FINDING A SOLUTION

When I gave up on finding a LinkedIn expert whose work I related to, I reviewed profiles of people I admired, connections, and anyone who seemed like they had their shit together. This was before I really understood just how deep the illusion of success that social media, including LinkedIn, could be. None of what I learned or tried to emulate felt right, either.

I am almost embarrassed to admit how many hours I spent revamping my profile over the years. Sometimes it was just trying to get under the 2600 character limit in the About or Experience sections. (Ugh. I *know*.) Other times it was crafting the precise wording that would magically get people to flock to my profile and immediately sign up to work with me. (Ugh. *I KNOW*.)

I try not to think of all the time I wasted on those fruitless efforts.

There's a children's cartoon character called "Bob the Builder." He always asks his team, "Can we fix it?" to which they respond, "Yes, we can!"

Let's just say that I was no Bob the Builder, because despite the endless "fixing" I did on my profile, it was clearly a resounding, "No, I can't!"

Don't get me wrong: in many ways, LinkedIn has been good to me. I made great connections, some of whom are now friends. People often commented about my "impressive" accomplishments. I even acquired clients through LinkedIn, although never because of the About section wording I lovingly agonized over.

But the truth is that I never felt great about my profile, and what success I had was inconsistent. I am sure it had more to do with my ability to network than anything else.

I wanted someone to tell me the best way to fill out my LinkedIn profile so that it made the most sense for me, helped me get my message out, and helped me consistently get clients. Otherwise, what's the point of being on LinkedIn?

Sound familiar?

IT'S A COMMON FEELING

If you're like most people, you probably aren't thrilled with your LinkedIn profile. You don't like your headline, aren't sure about your About section, and don't understand why a random landscape isn't enough in your banner, or whether you should include everything in your experience section. And you definitely aren't converting prospects by someone simply looking at your LinkedIn profile. Or in the case of career professionals and job seekers, finding jobs.

The truth is, not many people actually crush it on LinkedIn without doing a ton of networking or a high volume of cold pitches. (Honestly, I don't know any, but I don't want to say no one.) Even when this volume-based way of finding leads is effective, it is exhausting and expensive. And the only option seems like hiring someone to do your LinkedIn lead gen for you.

CRACKING THE CODE FOR LINKEDIN

I've been on LinkedIn for well over a decade, and during that time, my efforts to improve my profile and make LinkedIn work for me were half-assed at best because, dammit, there had to be a guru who could do this better than me.

It wasn't until 2023 when I fully gave up on finding the perfect LinkedIn "expert" to help me. Instead, I finally and fully committed to mastering LinkedIn myself. My goal was to get my profile to work for me—more than just being a beacon for a ton of cold pitches—and for my messaging to get people to say yes to my connection requests and get on a call with me.

I listened to podcasts, studied profiles, and then applied what I was learning. I kept what worked, and wasn't afraid to throw out what didn't.

I shared what I learned with friends and other folks in my network, usually after someone lamented that they didn't understand how to use LinkedIn or that they didn't like their profile. I'd do a quick profile review and point out ways to improve it. Almost immediately, they felt better about their profiles, and their audience responded better to them.

Then I heard from one of my early adopters who followed all of my recommendations to the letter. She'd received some unsolicited feedback; this person loved her LinkedIn profile and trusted that she'd do an excellent job on their project. She established trust *using only her LinkedIn profile.* She also noticed a significant uptick in connection requests and unsolicited discovery calls, which she directly attributes to her new-and-improved LinkedIn profile.

All this with no change in how she networked and engaged on LinkedIn.

It was at this point that I realized my formula really worked.

So what is the secret sauce? Strategy.

CHAPTER 3

Strategy

STRATEGY IS THE BIG BUZZWORD THESE DAYS. Every third consultant now calls themself a strategist and coaches who don't want to be called a coach do it, too. We now have marketing strategists, content strategists, sales strategists, and even corporate strategists.

Too bad many of them don't understand what strategy is. A quick conversation with many of them proves this to be true. I was on a call where the speaker, a self-identified marketing strategist, was using the words "positioning" and "strategy" interchangeably. One of the attendees finally asked the speaker what the difference was, and it was painful to witness because they clearly didn't know. I finally jumped in to explain the difference.

And this assault on strategy doesn't end with people misidentifying their roles and abilities. I lose the show every time I hear someone trying to sell a problem where they are selling us "the exact strategy that made me a million dollars in 10 days!" First, it's probably not true. Second, if everyone can use the exact same strategy and get the exact same results, it's probably not a real strategy.

Clearly, with all the misunderstanding around what strategy is, it's best we start by defining it.

WHAT IS STRATEGY?

Simply put, a strategy is a plan that takes you from where you are to where you want to be. It is how you reach your goal. However, a strategy takes into consideration all the resources and experiences that are available to that person or business.

That's the magic sauce of strategy: resources.

Resources can include money, experience, knowledge, people, location, physical assets, existing clients, market, market research, education, gender of players, and any number of things that can affect the outcome directly or indirectly.

Clearly, none of us have the exact same resources. For that reason, no two strategies will be exactly alike. That is why there is no such thing as a one-size-fits-all strategy, despite what the gurus say.

An example is helpful here. I live in Washington, D.C. Let's say I want to go across town. I can get there several different ways, including going through the national park. This is the shortest distance, but it's not always the fastest, and I want to get there as quickly as I can. I need to consider the day of the week, time of day, current weather, if it recently rained (parts of the road sometimes get closed off), whether we're driving or biking (the hills!), if there are any local events happening (which might close down a road), if we need to make any stops, and more.

In this example, my goal is to get across town as quickly as possible. To do that, I need a plan, which is where strategy comes in. My strategy is to take all the factors I've listed above into consideration to make that happen.

We all make these kinds of decisions all the time, often split-second and without much forethought. The point of this book is to help you do this with your LinkedIn profile, which is why you'll note that I talk a lot about the *goal* of your LinkedIn profile.

HOW STRATEGY IS RELEVANT TO CREATING A SUCCESSFUL LINKEDIN PROFILE

LinkedIn is a weird combination of personal branding and, for those of us who are founders and business owners, marketing our skills and businesses. Too personal, and no one knows what you do or what you're trying to sell. Too business-like, and no one gets to know you, which is what people want on LinkedIn.

The goal, of course, is to hit that middle area where you're interesting enough to get to know; and your profile is clear enough to share your offers so that people will buy from you or hire you.

The first you accomplish by engaging on LinkedIn. The second you accomplish by creating a kickass profile that works for you, which is what we cover in this book.

Keep in mind these two things as you navigate this book and revamp your profile:

1. **Always think of LinkedIn as a conversation, rather than a constant sales pitch.** What do you like to know when you meet someone? What kind of information do you like to share? What kind of people do you like to work with, and how do you make that decision?

   Understanding this framework will help you determine the best way to present the information in your profile. After all, if you were at a networking event, what is it that you want people to know? What can you say that will showcase what you do and how good you are at it? How do you keep your audience intrigued enough that they keep chatting with you?

2. **When you are planning out your LinkedIn profile, you need to be clear about your end goal.** Do you want to bring in clients? Become a thought leader? Find funding? Promote your business? Find a job? Whatever you decide is your primary goal should always be at the forefront of your mind as you decide what to include and how to position the experience and offers you have.

   Be sure to check out the chapter *How to Use This Book* for more details. Additionally, look for the chapter called *Profile Cheat Sheets*. You'll find a map of which sections you want to add to your profile based on your goals.

USING AI OR LLMS

With the massive proliferation of tools based on artificial intelligence or large language models, it's tempting to have one of these tools to create your entire LinkedIn profile for you and call it a day.

It is never a good idea to trust ANY of these models blindly, for many reasons.

Furthermore, sometimes the information is just plain inaccurate and ChatGPT has been known to make up citations and links that do not exist. I've heard stories, but it was only recently that I experienced it personally. I recently asked ChatGPT what the current building code is for determining the number of smoke detectors that should be in my home. ChatGPT responded by telling me that it couldn't tell me the building code for where I live (the building code is available online), that I needed to look it up myself, and then gave me a link for canivote.org.

This response made no sense. I'd never even asked ChatGPT any political questions, much less about voting, ever.

Then there is the question about your own voice and tone. Some people swear that their tools sound "just like" them, and maybe one day, this will be true. But as of the publishing of this book, most of us can still spot an AI-generated post or comment pretty easily.

However, I'd be a fool to think that anyone who reads this book will never use AI/LLMs to work on their LinkedIn profile. So, I decided to get ahead of the issue.

What AI/LLMs are useful for is brainstorming ideas and phrasing. To that end, the sections that might benefit from brainstorming help include prompts that you can input into your AI/LLM of choice, like ChatGPT. Pay close attention to the results that they generate and make sure the wording, voice, and structure reflect who you are and your personal style. You are not required to use any of them verbatim.

It will be useful to use the same thread/chat to ask your AI/LLM of choice for all the prompts, unless there is a significant change in your goal or approach for your LinkedIn profile. Doing this will allow the system to get to know you and apply information it already has for you.

You will find these prompts both in this book and on the book bonuses website. The prompts and wording of queries are changing all the time as these tools upgrade. The website will include the most recent recommended version, so be sure to check there. You can access them with the QR code.

NOTE: These prompts are designed for ChatGPT, but they also work well in Claude, Gemini, Copilot, and other AI/LLM models. To ensure best results, include your full context. When in doubt or if the model isn't returning results that work for you, add "Write this as if it was going on my LinkedIn profile." You can also give it detailed instructions. Detailed tweaks are available on in the book bonuses.

TIPS TO CRAFT A KICK-ASS LINKEDIN PROFILE

What follows are some tips that will aid you in crafting a LinkedIn profile that rocks.

Tip 1: Know your goal

I always tell my clients, "If you don't know where you're going, you're not going to end up where you want to be." This same advice applies to your LinkedIn profile. You need to know the goal or purpose for creating and maintaining your LinkedIn profile. Everything you do, how you say it, how you present it, hinges on this one thing.

This is why identifying how you want to use your LinkedIn profile is the single most important thing you can do to create a great LinkedIn profile that works for you.

For some of us, it's also one of the hardest things to do, too. It feels like a monumental, irrevocable decision. So for those of you who struggle with this, remember that you can always change it later. Pick one goal, usually the one that's most familiar, and update your profile with that in mind. When you're ready, you can adapt your profile to your new goal.

I have a client who has an in-person studio, a program she teaches, and is also becoming a thought leader. Conventional wisdom would suggest that she focus on the thought leadership role because it would bring people into her world, but that's newer and less familiar. The in-person studio is only local to her, so it doesn't make sense to focus on that. Instead, we decided on promoting her program. She'll be able to update her profile overall, then as she expands her role in thought leadership, she can update her Banner, Headline, About, and Featured sections.

You can also change your profile according to an immediate goal or if you have an event coming up. This is why I recommend creating what I like to call an "emotional support document." All those great words and phrases you came up with, or anything you may want to use later, can be added to your ESD.

Tip 2: Keep it short and sweet

LinkedIn now only shows the first two lines of any entry in most sections. To learn more, your audience needs to click through to see a full description. This is true regardless of whether you use many sections or just a few. That means that it's crucial to make those two lines impactful.

Additionally, with people's shortened attention spans, no-one reads long, rambling descriptions, no matter how beautifully written, poignant, accurate, or appropriate they are. That means that short-and-sweet is absolutely necessary for any of the written elements on your profile.

There's a quote I've seen that will inspire our modus operandi as we work on the different sections of our profiles.

- *Just because we can, doesn't mean we should...*
  use every character limit to the max.

- *Just because we can, doesn't mean we should...*
  include every experience we've ever had.

- *Just because we can, doesn't mean we should...*
  use every section available to us.

See a theme here? For founders and business owners, LinkedIn is not best used as a repository to dump everything you've ever done professionally. Frankly, this is true of career professionals and job seekers as well. Instead, the information should be kept relevant, impactful, and in as few words as possible. If it is none of those, don't include it.

Tip 3: Don't be humble

One of my favorite quotes comes from Kamala Harris during her 2024 run for president: "Not all of us are aspiring to be humble." I'd argue that most of us cannot afford to be humble, because no one is going to promote us like we can.

LinkedIn is a great opportunity to show off your accomplishments. Do not dim your light or underplay what you've accomplished. I've tried to provide parameters as to when it's appropriate to add an accomplishment, and it's generally based on timeframe, relevance, and whether it's an interesting story that can add depth to your profile.

For example, in graduate school, my team and I won several national competitive case competitions. This fact is neither timely nor relevant since I can point to more current examples that demonstrate what I've accomplished, such as advising a client from pivoting to funding in three months.

On the other hand, if I owned a patent for a piece of sports equipment, or lead firewalking retreats, then those could be worth including. They make me more interesting.

Tip 4: Don't overcomplicate what you do

Crafting "I help" statements in a specific formula and then using said "I help" statements everywhere is a trend that I really, really wish would die. The content is useful to help clarify your offer, because it includes what you do, how you do it, and who your ideal client is. However, sitting in networking events listening to people rattle off their "I help" statements is painful. More than half the time, I have no idea what the hell they were talking about.

Don't get me wrong: As an English major, words are my JAM. I love a clever turn of phrase and delight in listening to my Gen Z kids rattle off phrases I've never heard, trying to figure them out.

But in a business setting? Please don't make me work hard to figure out what you do. One man I knew rattled off his whole "I help" statement when we met. It took me a solid five minutes of asking questions about what exactly he did until I finally understood that he was a health insurance agent. If he'd told me, "I am a health insurance agent," I'd know and remember what he did. Instead, I lost five minutes of my life I'll never get back because he was more committed to that "I help" statement than making sure I clearly understood what he did.

Being able to share what you do concisely is a learned skill, and it takes practice. One technique I recommend to my clients is to set up a whole bunch of coffee chats (not for the purpose of selling anything) and explain what you do. You'll see what resonates and what doesn't. You'll also learn how to say what you do more concisely until it's short and direct.

Tip 5: Use color to amplify your profile

Using color as a component to your strategy is unusual, but it works. We don't think of LinkedIn as a colorful place. Sure, we see lots of photos in our feed, mostly of people standing in groups at an event. *yawn*

We see even less color on profiles. No banner, mostly dreaded gray boxes, more pictures of people standing around at conferences. Resumes can be more colorful than some LinkedIn profiles.

The good news, though, is that this gives you an opportunity to stand out from the crowd by leveraging color. Color, when used well, can capture the attention of your audience when they are glancing at your LinkedIn profile.

However, to bring in the wow factor, the key is to have your chosen color(s) be uniform and vibrant. It doesn't have to be your primary branding colors or hot pink (although hot pink is extremely effective), but the color should be deep enough to offset and be noticed among the standard black-and-white of a LinkedIn profile. Use one that contrasts nicely, like reds, blues, pinks, and teal. Skip the muted ones, like beige and lighter gray, dark green, and even some pastels.

Tip 6: Use uniform graphics

Have you ever encountered a brand that looks disjointed or inconsistent because their graphics don't match? It looks odd, it's disconcerting to the eye, and is terrible (and rarely memorable) branding.

The key is to create graphics that look like they match with the other graphics on the page, starting at your banner and moving down throughout your profile. The design doesn't need to be complicated or overly unique, but it does need to be consistent.

Whichever color and branding you choose is the color that you will repeat throughout your profile, starting at your Banner section and then the media in the Services, Featured, and even Experience sections. Anytime media are mentioned in each chapter, know that you want to design the graphics with those colors and some consistency in design.

The eye likes uniformity and is attracted to color, so take advantage of this.

Tip 7: Optimize your profile

Everything I share in this book will actively help you optimize your profile, but one the best thing you can do is to make sure that you use the right terminology so that you come up in the search engine, whether you are a founder or business owner, thought leader, career professional, or job seeker.

You can look up search terms or common SEO for your industry, or you can use an AI/LLM to look it up for you. To that end, this will be your first AI/LLM prompt recommendation:

I want to optimize my LinkedIn profile for visibility and relevance.

My goal for my LinkedIn profile is *[insert your goal, such as: get more clients / find a job / become a thought leader / sell my book]*.

I do work related to: *[insert main area(s) of expertise]*
My target audience is looking for: *[insert what people search for or need]*
I want to show up in searches related to: *[insert terms or roles]*
Give me a list of 20-30 keywords or phrases I should include in my profile.
Use a mix of common and niche terms, include both skills and results-based keywords.

Do you need any additional information from me?

Your AI/LLM tool will ask additional questions if it needs more information.

You can also ask the AI/LLM tool to review your LinkedIn profile (use the whole URL) and ask it what terms it thinks you need to include in your profile. That would be something like this:

Review my LinkedIn profile at **https://linkedin.com/in/YOURNAME**

I want to optimize my profile for visibility and relevance. What key terms am I missing based on your understanding of what I offer / what I do?

Give me a list of 20-30 keywords or phrases I should include in my profile.

Use a mix of common and niche terms, include both skills and results-based keywords.

Do you need any additional information from me?

Once you get those terms, review them closely because they may not make sense for you. Once you pick the ones that do make sense, pepper them throughout your profile, especially in your Headline, About, and Experience sections. If none of these are terms that don't naturally lend themselves to what is in your profile, simply list them at the bottom of your About section.

DEVELOPING YOUR LINKEDIN STRATEGY

As I explained earlier in this chapter, your strategy will be unique to you because it's based on your goals for your profile, your experience, and several other factors. However, there are common factors to the most successful LinkedIn profiles: they are concise, precise, and strategic in their approach.

Your LinkedIn profile is a key component of your personal branding. It is how people get to know you and decide whether to continue engaging. This is true whether you're a founder/business owner, or a career professional/job seeker.

As you craft and update your profile, take into consideration everything, from your goals to your audience, and then apply this approach to *every single part* of your LinkedIn profile.

CHAPTER 4

How To Use This Book

UPDATING YOUR LINKEDIN PROFILE can feel like a daunting task. For me, only writing a resume feels harder. Sure, there was that time that my task avoidance was so strong that I did my taxes and about 32 other outstanding administrative tasks before I finally did what I needed to do. But updating my LinkedIn profile often felt harder than that.

I don't want you to feel the same way. Statistically, though, you probably do. My goal with this book is to provide context and practical tips for creating your LinkedIn profile to one that you feel great about, and that converts.

In each chapter, you'll not only find instructions on how to approach and execute each section. In some cases, you can access full-color examples using the QR code at the end of this chapter and the end of the book.

This chapter addresses the best way to use this book.

IF YOU'RE A SEASONED LINKEDIN USER

Chances are that you are a seasoned LinkedIn user, however you're still likely to learn a few new things throughout the book. I'd recommend reviewing the chapter called *Strategy* to understand how this approach is different from what you've previously learned, and to review this chapter so that you understand how each chapter is organized. Then go to the last chapters, which are essentially cheat sheets. The chapter *What Goes Where* tells you the best place to store particular information. The chapter called *Profile Cheat Sheets* outlines which professions will most likely benefit from which sections, plus some ideas on positioning.

BEFORE YOU GET STARTED

I often say that every action starts with a decision, and that includes updating your LinkedIn profile. As a founder or business owner, there are three key decisions you need to make that will weave into nearly every aspect of your profile.

1. **What are you trying to accomplish with your profile?**
   Are you looking for clients? Gain exposure as a thought leader? Get funding for your business? Or something else? There is no wrong answer here.

2. **What are your products or offers?**
   You don't need to have this nailed down right away while you're working on the more generic parts of your business. But you will need this as you refine the sections that will do the heavy lifting for your LinkedIn profile pitch (and I don't necessarily mean selling).

3. **What is the tone and style of your brand?**
   You do not need to have a full branding board for this, but instead, understand how formal your industry is and the persona you plan to portray. Are you a super formal person, or more laid back? Are you a colorful and funky person, or more reserved? You may find that this changes as you work on your profile or your business evolves, but starting someplace will help.

FOLLOW THE DOPAMINE

There is no right or wrong order in which to set up your profile. The simplest way to get started on your LinkedIn profile is to do the sections that feel the least intimidating. If a section is already done (such as the Experience section), review that chapter in this book to see if the tips I've provided have motivated you to add some updates.

A few early wins will inspire you to keep moving forward.

LESS IS MORE

For some reason, we've all been taught to believe that we should use every available character LinkedIn allows us in every single field. That's rarely a good idea. Why? Think about the last time you read a 2600-character About section. Or each 2000-character description for each Experience section entry.

Chances are it's been a very long time, or never. This also means that few (if any) people are reading the long-ass descriptions in your profile.

People don't have time to wade through a white paper level of detail, so you need to figure out what to say in a more concise and clear way. When I say "in a couple sentences," I mean one or two sentences, not extended paragraphs.

CHAPTER LAYOUTS

Each chapter of this book is dedicated to a different section. Each chapter is also broken down into the following sections:

■ **Purpose of section**

The first part of each chapter explains the purpose, relevance, and context of each section, helping you understand how to use it effectively. The description is geared toward founders and business owners, however I've made a point to note how it can also be applied by career and other LinkedIn users.

■ **Career professionals and job seekers**

What to include in each section and how to do it very much depends on why you're using LinkedIn and your goals. Much of what I've shared in this book is geared toward founders and business owners, but career professionals and job seekers have also found this advice helpful. Each chapter has a section that tells you how to adapt your approach if you fall into the latter category.

■ **Strategy questions**

Next, you will find a few strategy questions to consider as you approach this section. These are helpful to keep in mind because what you include in each section will often be based on these questions.

■ **What to include in the section**

Most chapters offer a description of what to include in each section. Where relevant, I give examples.

■ **What to avoid in the section**

Most chapters also include a section on what *not* to include. These descriptions are based on real LinkedIn profiles I've reviewed and highlight what didn't work or what added value to a profile.

■ **How to format entries & other tips**

Some sections require a little more finesse, so the corresponding chapters will provide more details and considerations as you work through what to include and how to word it. Some chapters have an "In Summary" section, which gives a quick summary of do's and don'ts.

■ **Worksheets**

Some sections have worksheets that you can access through a QR code. These are meant to walk you through the process I use with my clients to create the wording for big-impact sections, like your Headline and About sections.

■ **AI/LLM Prompts**

Some sections include an AI/LLM prompt. These are designed to help you think through what you want to say and how you want to say it. Remember to review the results carefully so that it matches your tone. Also, confirm it says what you mean to say, and check the website for the most recent prompt. I wrote about this in the last chapter.

■ **Examples**

Some examples are provided in this book and others you can access through the QR code. You may find it helpful to check out the colors or layouts to help inspire you to create your own, such as the Banner and Featured sections.

■ **Action Plan**

I don't want you to have to make a plan of attack for each section, so each chapter ends with an action plan. This helps you knock out the corresponding section as easily and quickly as possible.

IT'S YOUR PROFILE, SO YOU GET TO MAKE ALL THE DECISIONS

My recommendations in this book are based on what I've seen work—and the disasters I've witnessed—after reviewing thousands of profiles. I've done the research and tested the results. I know what works for most founders and business owners, and it's the opposite of what most people do.

And then I applied what I've been doing for my clients, and again for career professionals and job seekers. I learned that this approach is also effective for that audience, too.

My goal is to help you understand each part, so you determine what works best for you. I want you to feel great about your LinkedIn profile, be proud of what you've accomplished, and excited about how you're sharing it with the world.

So regardless of what I share here, pick and include the sections that are important for your work, that feel good and right, and that work for your audience and industry.

Remember "follow the dopamine" above? A version of that applies here, too. If it doesn't work, try again. If you're not getting the responses you want, try something else. As long as you're engaging on LinkedIn with your peers and ideal clients, your profile views should be going up, you should be getting better connections, and you should have more opportunities.

One important caveat: don't be so entrenched in what you think you know that you aren't willing to adapt.

I had a client who was adamant that the language they used to describe what they do was exactly right. The problem is that it was exactly right 30 years ago, but the terminology had changed and using old terminology aged my client. When I pointed it out, they told me that they thought I was "splitting hairs" and it wouldn't make a difference. However, no one was looking for what they were offering using the old terminology—my client was literally the only person I could find on LinkedIn who did. I suggested that they look it up themselves and see how others are phrasing what they do, and my client finally changed it.

BONUSES

Be sure to use the QR code to check out the bonuses I've included online.

There, you will find:

■ Sample graphics

■ Sample sections

■ Worksheets

■ Review of a LinkedIn profile wireframe

Or find it at **https://loveyourlinkedinprofile.com/secret-book-bonuses**

ACRONYMS

When my kids were in middle school, they'd often lose the homework they finished before they turned it in. Out of desperation, I finally started putting those assignments in a large manilla envelope. My eldest complained that it was ugly, and that's how the UME ("ugly manilla envelope") was born. Teachers thought it was hilarious, and it worked. To this day, they will still ask for an UME (pronounced "OO-me").

In short, I'm a fan of using acronyms for phrases I repeat often, so here's a glossary of acronyms you'll see repeatedly through this book:

■ **DGB: Dreaded gray box** refers to any box on a LinkedIn profile missing a graphic. This can range from a banner with nothing on it to the little box down the left side of experience, education, volunteering, and a few others. Those small boxes can be clicked on to access the company pages for those organizations. You might think of them as where favicons or thumbnails go, and you'd be right. But while they are blank, we shall call them DGB. The goal is to have as few DGBs as possible.

■ **ESD: LinkedIn emotional support document** is a document where you add all the information you used to have on your LinkedIn profile. Many of us can't just delete what we used to have on our LinkedIn profiles, so I recommend creating what I call an emotional support document (or a folder, if that makes more sense). You may never use the old phrasing you had to describe the details of your work, but you'll feel better knowing it's somewhere you can access.

■ **ICP: Ideal client profile** refers to your ideal client or audience. These are the decision-makers in your world. They are the ones who will decide to buy from your company. Sometimes, they are consumers and end users; other times, they fill a specific role in a larger company. Sometimes, they are referred to as ICAs or ideal client avatars.

■ **KPI: Key performance indicators** are the quantifiable metrics that measure the goals achieved. These are often set by an organization, individuals, or department, but as a founder or business owner, these might be the metrics you've achieved in your business overall, such as "30% growth annually."

CHAPTER 5

Banner

THE BANNER SECTION is the big area at the top of your profile, behind your profile headshot. Think of it as the billboard to your whole profile. While your headline first entices people to check out your profile, your banner is the first opportunity to really impress your audience enough that they want to keep exploring it.

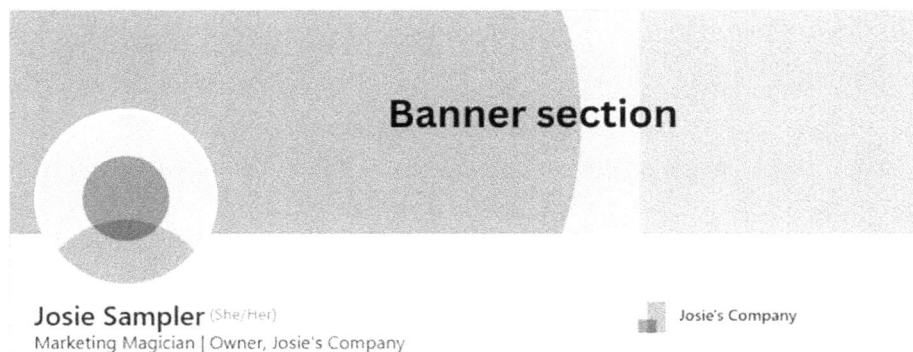

Despite it being the most valuable real estate on a LinkedIn profile, it is probably the most under-appreciated and under-utilized section.

Too many banners are left blank, leaving the audience to view a massive DGB (dreadful gray box). Another popular feature is landscape pictures, which—while a slight improvement over the DGB—is a complete waste for founders and business owners because it's a lost opportunity to get your audience interested in you. This chapter aims to fix this problem.

CAREER PROFESSIONALS AND JOB SEEKERS

Everything in this section applies to you the same way it does business owners, and tidbits specifically for career professionals and job seekers can be found throughout. Follow guidelines below, but keep in mind your potential employers rather than your ideal clients.

STRATEGY QUESTIONS

The strategy questions aim to help you determine the goal of this section and what to include.

- What is the transformation I provide?
- What does it look like when I've been successful for or with my client?
- What is my genius? My area of expertise?
- What is my ICP (ideal client profile) looking for?
- Which of my branding colors is vibrant enough to be reused throughout my profile?

WHAT TO INCLUDE IN YOUR BANNER SECTION

Your banner is where you get to invite people into your world, and the most effective way to do this is not by asking questions or by listing your list of services. Questions lead to uncertainty and a list of services can be presumptuous.

Instead, it is by making a declarative statement, which usually falls into one of two categories: You either describe what success looks like for your ICP or you describe your genius/area of expertise. And you do it in as few words as possible.

The goal is for your audience to quickly get the gist of your message, so that they are then sufficiently intrigued to keep moving through your profile. This is similar to a title or headline. It doesn't need to be a complete sentence—in most cases, it should not be a complete sentence—but it does need to give an accurate idea of what your audience can expect from you.

As you get ready to design your banner, consider adding the following elements:

- **Limited color palette.** You are under no obligation to use every single color in your branding color palette on your banner. In fact, it's probably better that you don't. Limited colors make a bigger impact. Single, solid colors or a gradient of the same color work well. If your background color is too busy because you use too many, then your message may be hard to see.

- **Vibrant color.** This does not necessarily mean you should use neon pink (although that's a very effective color). As I explain in the chapter, *Strategy*, you want to use a strong, vibrant color that you will continue to use throughout your LinkedIn profile for the thumbnails and graphics. Solid dark colors can work with white or cream font or as stripes in your other graphics. The goal is consistency of color that ties back to your banner.

- **Large, bold font.** While the font does not need to take up all the available space of your headline, it must be readily visible and legible. That means certain stylistic fonts (such as skinny fonts) may not work because they are too hard to read. To review how your chosen style works, you can always upload it and review it on the LinkedIn app as well as desktop.

- **Initial or sentence capitalization.** Words that are all capitalized tend to be harder to read, so double-check to see if your font is easily legible from a distance or at a glance. Most are not, so capitalizing only the first letter of each word or the first letter of the first word makes sense.

- **Your logo, but small.** If you want to include your logo—and it's completely reasonable to do so—make sure the logo is considerably smaller than anything else on the banner. A good rule of thumb is that it's at least small enough to fit above your profile picture (the circle), even if you don't include it there. Your logo should not be the focal point of your banner.

- **Clear messaging.** I often see banners that use a clever turn of words or say something interesting, but I still have no clue what that person offers in terms of expertise or transformation. Whatever you say, make sure that it does not require added context to make sense.

- **Concise messaging.** Use as few words as possible. There is simply not enough room to include everything you could possibly want to share. Your goal is to make your message interesting enough that someone wants to continue exploring your LinkedIn profile.

- **A promise.** As noted above, an effective banner will have a declarative statement that is a promise. That promise is the transformation you provide or one that clearly identifies your skillset. Either way, you want your audience to think, "Oh, I want what they are promising."

  A call-to-action (CTA) can also be effective here, but only if it can also be interpreted as a promise. For example, "Get fit now" is both a promise and a CTA. "Buy now" is only a CTA. CTAs are best used for limited-time promotions. (See below for more details.)

- **A philosophy or approach.** If you are a career professional or job seeker, the banner is an opportunity to share what makes you great at your job or what you think is important about what you do. The key here is to focus on you, not your specific job description or what your company does. In short, what do you bring to the table? It's not a call-to-action, but it does give your audience an idea about what to expect of you.

- **Right-justify.** Right-justify your message as much as possible. This is because the profile picture/headshot overlaps the left side of the banner, so if your message is centered on the banner, it could overlap on the left side.

- **Picture of your product.** If you sell a physical product, it is appropriate to add a picture of that product, but only if it is a physical product.

- **Logos of places you've been published or seen.** If you're a thought leader and would like to highlight some of the places you've been featured, then adding those logos might be something worth doing as they act as endorsements. However, they should not take center stage or detract from your own message, which usually means they are much smaller and sometimes faded out. A line of logos along the bottom works well, for example.

- **Full or half-body photo of you.** Adding your own picture to the banner can be effective if it is part of the graphic and isn't the only background. (See below for the "no photos" recommendation.) This is no longer a popular thing to do, but when done right, it can work well. Note, though, that these are not usually the same exact photo as the one you use for the profile headshot (but the same photo shoot is fine).

In short, your banner should be a brief but impactful message in a color that stands out against the black-and-white background of LinkedIn, with a font that is easily readable. Your goal is to make people interested enough in what you offer that they keep checking out the rest of your profile.

WHAT TO AVOID IN YOUR BANNER SECTION

The Banner section should never be left blank. If you are in a rush, at the very least create a banner that's a solid color and add your tagline. That should not be your final version, though.

Meanwhile, here are some things you do **not** want to include in your banner:

- **Photos with no context.** I know this is an unpopular take because a few years ago, everyone was recommending that you put a photo of yourself speaking at an event or winning an award or something. But the truth is that photos without words or context do not help your audience decide to work with you, even if it's a great picture of you. They don't even inspire people to keep checking out your profile.

- **Group photos.** If you still insist on using a photo (see above), then know that a group photo is probably even less of a good idea, so skip those. Your face is likely too small to see and it's often hard to figure out what the group photo was for.

- **Only your logo or company name.** Absolutely be proud of yourself for starting your business, but remember that chances are that no one knows the name of your company or recognizes your logo. Don't waste this space to only show that off. Your logo, if you decide to include it, should be relatively small, no larger than the space above your profile headshot.

- **Your employer's logo.** This is relevant for anyone who is using their LinkedIn profile for both a primary job and your own business. Your employer neither needs nor deserves your valuable real estate. The exception is for people who work in sales on behalf of the company and use their profile for this purpose. However, in most cases, put yourself first.

- **Too many graphics.** If your banner is too busy, you force people to concentrate too hard. Your audience will be confused. And confused people do not buy. You do not want them to overpower your message. So if you use any graphics, keep them to a minimum and keep them away from your messaging.

- **Irrelevant graphics or information.** Skip the irrelevant graphics if they do not add to your message. The exception might be a full body shot of you, but other cartoons and such? Unnecessary and confusing.

- **Questions.** Your banner is not the start of an engagement post, so don't put your key engagement question front and center. You do not want people questioning why they are on your page. You want them to want to get to know you. Answering questions takes effort and at that point you haven't yet earned the right to ask them any questions.

- **All caps.** All caps can be hard to read, especially if the font is narrow and/or the letters are close together. Stick to initial caps or sentence cap (first letter of a word is capitalized).

HOW TO DESIGN YOUR BANNER

As you get ready to design your banner, know that the banner for your personal LinkedIn page and your company page are two different sizes. You can create the banner in an app like Canva or Snappa, both of which have free versions.

Note that the sizes and requirements change from time-to-time, so be sure to check your banner occasionally to make sure that everything you want visible is still visible. You should do this from a visitor perspective and not your own.

The wording for your banner is often the most challenging part. What you want to say is the thing that provides an overview of what you do or the transformation that someone experiences. One way to do this is to write down everything you do, look for the theme, and then play with the words until you get to the heart of it. You can use your "help statement," if you have one, as a starting point. However, help statements are usually too wordy and cumbersome for a banner. Your tagline only works if it's understood without providing context.

As you put together the different elements of your banner, remember that it should be clean, uncluttered, and easy to read.

Finally, and most importantly, be sure to view your banner on both desktop and mobile (as a viewer, not as you). Too often, the font is too small or delicate to read on mobile or it gets blocked by the profile headshot.

WHEN YOU ARE PROMOTING A TIME-SENSITIVE OFFER

Your banner is an excellent place to share a time-sensitive offer, such as a program, course, book, or anything else with an end date. You can easily borrow language and graphics from your offer's landing page, often similar to the banner you have there. You will need to reformat it.

If you are promoting a book or something with a specific graphic, remember that viewers might not be able to see the title of your book clearly. Or maybe you have a clever title but the topic is not obvious. In that case, your LinkedIn profile should make it clear what your book or program is about.

IF YOU PAY FOR LINKEDIN PREMIUM BUSINESS

If you have a Premium Business subscription, you now have the option of including up to five banners, which rotate every three seconds, like a dynamic carousel. This may be useful if you are a business owner who is also an author and/or wants to be a thought leader. Career professionals can use it to highlight philosophy, company you work for and position, and thought leader credentials. Or someone like me, who is a business strategist who also teaches cybersecurity webinars for humans, has a Substack account with several publications, and also published a book, proving she's an expert on LinkedIn.

Very few subscribers are taking advantage of this, so I'm not sure if this feature will be effective or popular enough for people to look for it. However, keep this option in mind if you're already paying for Premium Business.

AI/LLM PROMPT

Remember to check the website for the most recent version.

> I'm designing a banner for my LinkedIn profile. Give me a list of short, powerful phrases or taglines that could go on it.
>
> My goal for my LinkedIn profile is *[insert your goal, such as: get more clients / find a job / become a thought leader / sell my book]*.
> My work focuses on *[insert what you do or stand for]*.
> I want the banner to communicate *[choose: a key belief / a bold result / my audience's biggest problem / what makes me different]*.
>
> Tone: *[insert tone — e.g., confident, rebellious, warm, visionary]*
> Limit the options to 4-8 words each. Make them clear, memorable, and compelling.
>
> Do you need any additional information from me?

SAMPLE BANNER SECTIONS

Use QR code found in Chapter 4 and at the end of the book to see sample Banner sections.

ACTION PLAN

Ready to dive in? The Action Plan is what you need to do to implement this section.

☐ Pick a background color that meets the suggestions above.

☐ Brainstorm language for your messaging. Remember, no questions!

☐ Pick a font that is easily visible and readable.

☐ Design your banner on Canva, Snappa, or a similar app. Remember that you will use this same or similar style for other graphics on your LinkedIn profile (such as for services, featured, volunteering, and projects).

☐ Save your banners as you create them so that you can switch them out later.

CHAPTER 6

Profile Headshot

IF YOU DON'T HAVE A HEADSHOT for your LinkedIn profile, it's time to get over yourself and get one ASAP. I don't care what your excuse is, how much you hate cameras, or how unphotogenic you think you are. Besides, you're probably wrong about being unphotogenic. And even if you're not, so what?

More importantly, according to LinkedIn, people with a profile picture are more likely to have their connection requests accepted and to be invited to connect. So that also means making your profile picture public to everyone, not just your connections.

Besides, having no profile picture is a red flag that screams, "SCAMMER." And if you're reading this, you're probably not a scammer.

Please review this chapter carefully. It's short, but considering the number of bad profile pictures on LinkedIn, it's clearly necessary information.

CAREER PROFESSIONALS AND JOB SEEKERS

Everything in this section applies to you the same way it does business owners. Follow the guidelines below.

STRATEGY QUESTIONS

- In my industry, how formal are headshots expected to be?
- Does my current headshot give the impression I want to give?

ONE IS BETTER THAN THREE

This isn't Facebook or Instagram, so please stop with the multi-person shots for your profile picture. It should only be a picture of your head, not you and your baby, you and your spouse, you and a couple of friends, or even you and your dog.

We just want to see you. You and your beautiful smile are plenty.

FORMAL HEADSHOTS AREN'T ALWAYS NECESSARY, BUT YOU STILL NEED A HEADSHOT

Remember those terrible school pictures growing up? It always amazed me just how bad they were. I am pretty sure most of us were traumatized on some level by them.

(Side note: This photo trauma is real and still vivid decades later. Several of the beta readers of this book were compelled to share just how bad their pictures were, which included crooked bangs, very red pimples, and goofy, gummy smiles. I'm sorry if you also experienced this, but you still need to get over yourself and post a headshot.)

The good news is that LinkedIn is no longer as formal as it once was. While certain industries may warrant a formal headshot (corporate, consulting, and government are the most obvious), those headshots don't need to be reminiscent of our awful school pictures. A great photographer can capture a lot of personality and a moment of joy that makes you look gorgeous and approachable. When picking out a photographer, be sure to check out their portfolio, especially if you have more melanin in your skin. (IYKYK.)

TIP: Some networking events will feature a photographer doing professional headshots for a discounted price.

If you don't have the time or money for a formal headshot, you can crop a photo of yourself where you look great, which sends a similar message. Just make sure the background is light and not distracting. You can always use Canva or a similar app to remove the background and pick a color that reflects your brand or personality.

HEADSHOT—IT'S IN THE NAME

I recently saw a profile headshot of someone squatting. They looked like a hot pink frog and I couldn't make out their face.

The upshot is this: we love that you love to ski, but a profile picture of you skiing doesn't do much for us. Ditto with artistic compositions. Save those for your TikTok profile picture.

Those full-body poses? Not necessary. Chest and shoulders? Nope. Remember, headshot refers to HEAD. That's the part of your body above your neck.

Those little profile pictures are super small, with just enough room for your head.

Quick tip

If you market your products or services on multiple social media platforms, it's helpful to keep your profile picture the same across platforms. This makes it easier to find you.

IN SUMMARY

Headshots should meet the following criteria:

- Include only yourself. Really.
- Include only your head or head and shoulders.
- It should be mostly your head, centered, not offset in an artistic pose.
- Use a bright background that is contrasting but not distracting.
- Smile or present another expression that looks like you're having fun.
- Consider investing in a professional headshot. They are not essential, but a great one will make you feel fabulous.
- If you don't have a professional headshot, then make sure the photo meets the criteria listed here.

ACTION PLAN

If you have a great HEADshot in your profile picture, skip this section. If not:

☐ Decide what kind of message you want to send with your profile picture.

☐ Find a picture that meets the criteria listed above.

☐ For professional headshots, find a photographer whose style you love, makes you feel safe, and can bring out your best smile.

CHAPTER 7

Name

THE NAME SECTION is part of the intro header, and it is one of the first things that people see, so it is getting its own chapter. Also, when I refer to the Name section as "name," note that I am not referring to your actual, government name, but rather what you include on that line. (I discuss this below.)

Shakespeare's Juliet waxed, "What's in a name? That which we call a rose, By any other name would smell as sweet." This may be true for roses, but that doesn't mean that we can't take advantage of how our name is presented on LinkedIn. In fact, you might be surprised at how often it is necessary.

There are over one billion users on LinkedIn, and your name is just one of the factors that you can use to make yourself stand out and be memorable.

CAREER PROFESSIONALS AND JOB SEEKERS

Everything in this section applies to you the same way it does business owners. Follow the guidelines below.

STRATEGY QUESTIONS

- Does my industry expect formality?
- Is there a message I want to convey with my name or what's included on the name line?
- How do I want others to address me?

WHICH NAME SHOULD YOU USE?

In certain industries, formal names are imperative, but this is happening less frequently. In fact, LinkedIn is becoming less formal overall.

Remember, LinkedIn is not a resume. It's a networking tool, so how would you introduce yourself at a networking event?

Some thoughts:

■ If your government name is Michael but you prefer to be called Mike, then use Mike.

■ If your government name is Michael and only your close friends and colleagues use Mike, then use Michael.

■ If appropriate, use your name as a litmus test. For example, a woman with a two-name first name can weed out connections this way. People who don't know her personally will call her "Sarah Ann," but her friends and colleagues will call her Sarah.

YOUR STYLE IS YOUR BRAND

There are several little things you can do to make your name stand out. Some of these are reviewed here.

■ **Emojis can add pizzazz & send messages.** A well-placed emoji can add a little something to the Name section, either before or after your name or both. However, you might consider your industry and role before using them in your name because they send a particular message. For example, if you see someone using the Pride flag with their name, you can probably assume they are LGBTQIA+-friendly. I know folks who've used emojis successfully, but none were in a traditional corporate setting.

■ **Capitalization is optional but generally recommended.** bell hooks, wili.i.am, and e.e. cummings are all well known for their lack of capitalization in their names. If this is part of your brand or you have a reason for doing it this way, then of course, keep doing it. However, there are easier ways to be memorable. Make sure it matches your brand rather than be a cutesy gimmick.

- **Consider where your audience resides.** You may want to follow the conventions that your audience recognizes. Examples include:

  - **Alphabet.** If your audience resides in English-speaking countries, using the Latin alphabet often makes the most sense.

  - **Order of names.** In some cultures, it is common to put the family name first, which is the opposite of English-speaking countries.

- **Including degrees and certifications can be beneficial but isn't required.** In some professions (especially financial ones), this lets people know you have certain qualifications. My decision to add my degrees after my name (MBA, MA) is a result of learning how differently I was treated when folks realized I had those degrees. Somehow, what I was saying before they knew I had those degrees was suddenly deemed more legitimate. It's ridiculous, but since I work with founders and business owners, it carries weight. If I were an artist with an MBA, I probably wouldn't add that to my name. Finally, don't add that you received your MBA with distinction or where you went to school. I wouldn't even do that if you're a recent graduate. You can share that in your Experience section.

  If it makes sense for you, only add a master's degree or higher. Bachelor degrees are the bare minimum in many industries.

  Whatever you decide to do, stick to post-nominals that people know. Having an alphabet soup of post-nominals can make things confusing.

- **Honorifics aren't usually recommended but are sometimes necessary.** The problem with honorifics is that when someone calls themself "Dr. Kristina Jones," we don't know what kind of doctor they are (PhD, MD, DC, ND, etc.). Including both ("Dr. Kristina Jones MD") is technically redundant. That said, I've seen women do this more often than men because it puts their accomplishments front and center. Not surprisingly, they are usually in male-dominated fields. Their reason for adding the "Dr." in front of their name is similar to why I've added "MBA, MA" to the end of mine. We all gotta do what we gotta do.

■ **Say what you do.** Some folks add what they do to their name so that it shows up immediately after their name. There is definitely some value in certain circumstances, especially in standing out and making yourself memorable. An example is "Kristina Jones ~ TikTok Master." If Kristina is active on LinkedIn, even just in the comments, people will associate her with TikTok, and when they are ready to launch their TikTok account, they'll think of her. I know people who've used this technique to great success, but it's also possible that it's effective because not many people use it.

YOU MAY BE KNOWN BY SEVERAL NAMES

Many of us have gone by different names throughout our lifetimes. Maybe you decided that you didn't like the name you grew up with, so now you're using your middle name or a nickname. Or you changed your last name when you got married or divorced. Or maybe you went on an ayahuasca retreat last summer and your spirit guides insisted on a name change. It doesn't matter why; it only matters that you want people who knew you by your previous name to be able to find you.

LinkedIn now has a feature that allows you to add an additional name. This is where you would put that alternative name. You can choose whether that name is visible on your profile, but even if it's not, your profile will show up in searches. That means that if someone types in your alternate name, your profile will come up, but they won't see that name in your Name section. (You can also have the alternative name visible to everyone.)

Another idea is to put that alternative name in the About section, but you don't need to explain why. This could be useful if you've changed your name for any reason.

SAY MY NAME, SAY MY NAME

If your name is Alan or Sam or Kristen, there are generally only so many ways that your name can be pronounced. This tool may not be for you. But for many other people, it can be a good idea to add pronunciation, especially if you have an international network of people who speak multiple languages. Assume nothing.

PRONOUNS ARE YOUR FRIEND

When I launched a community for female and non-binary founders, I prepped to send out invites by sorting the founders in my network by gender as best I could. If the name was ambiguous or unfamiliar, I did a little research.

I thought I did well. I knew there were lots of names that were traditionally male names that are mostly female today, including Lindsay, Ashley, Carrol, Stacy, and Terry. And there are names that are less common but are used by multiple genders. But I was absolutely confident that the name "Joy" is only a female name. I found out the hard way that it is not.

I can handle the embarrassment of being wrong (that's not the only one I screwed up), but I don't want to make someone else uncomfortable by misgendering them. It takes only a few seconds to add pronouns to your profile, and it gives your network a little more information about you, especially with the ease of connecting with people all over the world.

Besides, LinkedIn has probably already gendered you. (No, I'm not kidding. Check your security settings and the data LinkedIn is collecting on you.) Why not clarify this for the world to see?

Now, if there was only some way for me to stop getting DMs and emails addressed to "Sir."

NOTE: I understand that some people, especially trans folks, might not want to use this feature for various reasons. Like everything else in this book, these are my thoughts and if it doesn't work for you, don't use it.

GETTING CLEVER WITH PRONOUNS (PLEASE DON'T)

In the pronouns section, you can pick He/Him, She/Her, They/Them or custom.

I've seen a man recently take the custom option and put his job title instead. I'm a big fan of breaking rules and expectations, but I am generally not a fan of this. I wouldn't want people to skip the pronouns in favor of job titles since there are so many other opportunities to show off what you do. Plus, the pronoun field has a very practical application that helps people understand how to interact with you.

ACTION PLAN

☐ Understand how formal your industry is.

☐ Explore adding more than your name to the Name section.

☐ If you have an alternative name and you want folks to find you by that name, consider adding your other name to the "Additional name" field.

☐ Consider adding the pronunciation of your name.

☐ Add your pronouns. PLEASE add your pronouns.

CHAPTER 8

Headline

WE EACH HAVE THAT ONE THING in our lives that is so agonizing that doing taxes or experiencing dental work without anesthesia seems comparatively enticing. For me, that's doing a resume. But a close second was writing a headline that I felt good about and that says what I want it to say without being too wordy. Fortunately, I figured out the latter.

The reason the headline is so hard is because of how important it is. People make several split-second decisions before they decide to click on your profile. The most important factor is based on what your headline says, possibly outside of where they came across you. And since LinkedIn only shows the first 40-50 characters of a headline preview, there's not a lot of space in which to do it.

It's a lot of pressure, for sure.

The good news is that this chapter (and accompanying worksheets) will help you create a headline that accomplishes what you want it to do.

NOTE: The headline section is part of the intro header, and it is arguably the thing that makes people want to check out the rest of your profile (aside from your witty engagement in the comments section of someone else's post). It is also one of the hardest sections to get right for yourself and your audience. So for these reasons, it's getting its own chapter.

CAREER PROFESSIONALS AND JOB SEEKERS

Most of the guidelines in this section apply to you the same way it does business owners. However, you may benefit from also stating your job title or something comparable so that your audience understands what you do. It is also acceptable to note temporary requests, such as if you're looking for a job, like "looking for my next opportunity" or "considering project management positions in the tech industry."

STRATEGY QUESTIONS

- What am I trying to accomplish with my profile?
- Is my focus on achievements or skillset?
- What does my audience consider credibility?
- Why should anyone hire me?
- Is it clear what I do, what I offer, or what I am looking for by reading my headline?

APPROACH TO WRITING YOUR HEADLINE

I advocate an approach to writing headlines that is somewhat unconventional, in part because I'm about to say something here that will get many marketers up-in-arms: I really, really do not like "I help" statements in headlines (or almost anywhere public, to be honest). I'm talking about the formula that is some variation of "I help <ICP> with <transformation> using my <secret formula for success>.

Don't get me wrong: I think "I help" statements are useful for figuring out those details. And they are definitely useful in helping you flush out your headline. But as a headline itself? It's often too long, too unwieldy, and takes up valuable real estate. If you really want to use it in your profile, it's usually best to save it for your About or Experience sections.

The other problem I frequently see with headlines is there will be a long list of accomplishments and accolades but no mention of what they do. I'm happy for you that you've mentored youth, won a 30-Under-30 award, are a 3x founder, are a top 100 influencer, are a top 1000 professional, were a contributor for several magazines (all listed), and want to share your tagline. It's seriously impressive...but what do you DO? Why should I hire you?

Unless you are well-known for what you do, limit the accolades and focus on making a compelling argument about why I should hire you. And do it in as few words as possible.

Finally, start to think of your ICP less in terms of demographics and more in terms of outcome desired. That's not to say you shouldn't consider demographics (say, if you prefer to work with female solopreneurs), but rather, as you craft your headline, focus on the people who will resonate with your authentic message rather than a much wider audience.

Ultimately, your headline needs to be easy to read and understood as quickly as possible. That usually means short, sweet, and impactful.

WHAT TO INCLUDE IN YOUR HEADLINE SECTION

It is tempting to throw everything important into the headline. After all, we want to **prove** how great we are and why someone should hire us or our company. However, in the "less is more" vein of thinking, too much is overwhelming, so it's important to be discerning about what we include.

This is why deciding the purpose of your LinkedIn profile is so important. The strategy for your header will differ depending on what you want to accomplish with your profile.

Following are some ideas and approaches to what to include. This list is not meant to be a comprehensive list of everything you should feature. Instead, it's an explanation of how to approach what you choose to include.

- **Back up your assertions. What you say in your headline MUST be reflected somewhere in your profile.** If you say you're a founder, then make sure that one of your experience entries is that of a founder. If you claim 30-Under-30 status, be sure that the details of that honor are listed below, including why and any links.

- **Tell us what you do.** Too often, we see headlines that are long and detailed…and yet we still have no idea what they do. (Seriously. Check out a bunch of headlines and see if you understand what they do.) "Founder, <YOUR COMPANY>" says nothing if no one knows what your company does. Skip the name and focus on what your audience needs to know. Or add your company name a little later in your headline.

- **Keep the messaging aligned with your end goal.** If you are looking for clients, tell them what they need to know to book a call with you. If you are growing your role as a thought leader, then credibility is key. If you're looking for funding, understand what's important for investors to know about you and your company.

- **Keep accolades current.** Accolades and awards can provide a level of credibility that you can't get elsewhere. At some point, though, they could sound dated. Touting that 30-Under-30 award when you're well into your mid-30s or later is not a good look. A TEDx talk achievement, though, lasts much longer.

- **Be descriptive so your audience self-selects.** The language and phrasing you use here will attract your audience. For example, if you call yourself a serial entrepreneur or 3x founder, the audience who wants to be connected with people with business experience will want to connect.

- **Be authentic.** Few of us are naturally formal all the time, so be authentic in what you say and how you say it. The energy behind the words makes a difference to who they resonate.

- **Quirky is good.** If you have space, it's not just fun but also a good strategy to include something that makes you, *you*. This makes you memorable and gives folks a place to start a conversation. The person who self-identifies as a meme queen and proves it by posting memes once a week will draw people in who like memes. I've met a mother of wolves, a queen of joy, and a professional doodler.

- **Use an icon or emoji to separate each "section" of your headline.** People skim in snippets, so keeping it short is great. Separating those snippets is important. The most popular ones are the vertical pipe (|), the bullet point, and the tilde (~).

WHAT TO AVOID IN YOUR HEADLINE SECTION

What to not include here is nearly as important as what to include. Some folks really work to maximize all 220 characters, and it shows, but not in a good way. The fact is that too much is overwhelming and distracting.

- **Website addresses.** There are so many opportunities to include live links in your LinkedIn profile. Why include a URL that requires someone to copy and paste? Don't do that because they rarely do. Instead, add it immediately below your headline. (See Header chapter for how.)

- **Emojification.** I am all for using a few well-placed emojis and odd punctuation in a headline, but too many can make it hard to read or look like AI created it. Also, emojis are hard for people who use screen readers because they are not accessible. So, be very deliberate if you use emojis in your headline.

- **Complete "I help" statements.** I know they are all the rage in certain circles, but they don't work in headlines. First, you're using up valuable real estate (the first 40-50 characters). Second, no one wants to read a complete sentence. Instead, use your "I help" statement to inspire your headline. (See above and worksheet.)

- **Redundancy.** Don't repeat what's easily found in multiple places. If you're the director of your company, it'll show up to the right of your headline, in your About section, in your experience section, and possibly in Services and Featured sections. It may not be necessary to include it in your headline.

- **Connection count.** This isn't the flex some people think it is, and if you're using LinkedIn right, this number will always change. Don't add this to your headline. It's the least interesting thing about you, and also irrelevant to everything you do and offer.

- **Questions.** Skip the questions. Your LinkedIn headline is not the start of an engagement post. This is the introduction part of a sales pitch, simply letting people know if they are even checking out the right person.

- **Your alma mater.** I recently saw a headline that stated "Harvard MBA." My first thought was, "So what?" My second was, "How pretentious." Perhaps that will benefit them, but unlikely, so skip it.

- **Capitalization.** Go easy on the initial caps. (The initial cap is capitalizing the first letter of a word.) Your headline isn't a book title, so if it's easier to read by only adding an initial cap to the first word, then do that. And don't use ALL CAPS. No one likes to get yelled at, even if you're excited.

- **Less is more.** Using all 220 characters available in your headline is a temptation usually best resisted. Long headlines are often too wordy or too confusing.

- **But not too little.** I once read a headline that simply said, "Chief Executive Officer." That's all, not even "CEO." It was a new company that he recently founded. Anyone can call themselves a CEO, but it means nothing on its own. Context is key, so give us enough to understand a bit about you and what you do.

HOW TO FORMAT YOUR HEADLINE SECTION

Remember, the goal of your headline is to be interesting enough that someone decides to open your profile. And then even more interesting so that they engage with your profile. This is a heavy load for so few characters, so you will have to be deliberate in your phrasing.

Furthermore, it is important to remember that the headline is about you and what you can do for your prospective clients. Or, if your goal is not necessarily to gain new clients, it's to let people know what you do. You want someone to read your headline and think, "This person can help me solve a problem I have." Or, "This person is someone I want in my network for a specific reason."

The headline should not be treated like the start of an engagement post. Do not ask questions. Do not make the type of declarative statements you can put in your banner. This is about you and what you bring to the table.

Know that the techniques I'm sharing here are not the only variations. In fact, I've seen several formulas for crafting the "perfect" LinkedIn headline and none of them made me excited to implement them.

The outline below is meant to give you guidelines to what could work for you, and it should absolutely not be considered carved in stone. Sometimes, a really effective headline is super short and tells a lot of information. Use the QR code near the Action Plan to access examples and why they work or don't work.

Note that you may need to try several headlines before you decide *this* is the one.

■ **In the beginning**

When you see a LinkedIn profile preview, you don't see someone's full headline, only the first 40-50 characters.

Check the "More profiles for you" section to the right of your LinkedIn profile, or go to My Network (at the top) and scroll down to "People you may know" for examples. (Note that as LinkedIn evolves, these sections may change names, but the purpose is the same.)

The first step is making those first 40-50 characters count. When you start with an "I help" statement, your first seven characters plus however many you need to describe your audience are wasted (remember that LinkedIn considers each space a character). So, "I help entrepreneurs" uses the first 21 characters of the preview. And you haven't even described what you do yet or given them a taste of what they can get by connecting with you.

Starting with a litany of titles (CEO, Founder, and Managing Director of My Company) isn't any better because they also take up a lot of space but offer no information that tells me your profile is worth engaging.

Therefore, this first section should start with the meaty stuff upfront, describing what you bring to the table, preferably with context clues so that someone who reads it wants to further explore what you do and can see themself in your world of influence.

■ **In the middle**

If the first part of your headline doesn't clearly show who would benefit from your services, use the middle section to identify them. Stay concise.

Alternatively, this could be an opportunity to add other means of credentialing your claims, such as "featured in Forbes" or "3x Founder + 2x Exit."

- ▪ **At the end**

  If you used the middle section for identifying your ICP, then you can use the end section to add credentialing and accolades. However, you can also add something interesting or unique about you that people might find interesting, fun, or that they might think is cool. For example, "meme queen" or "marathon runner" or "mother of wolves."

AI/LLM PROMPT

NOTE: Adjust this prompt to meet your goal. Also, note that ChatGPT, at least, likes to insert a lot of emojis, even if you ask it not to. You may need to delete a few or all of them.

> Help me write a compelling LinkedIn headline that combines what I do with something unexpected or distinctive.
>
> My goal for my LinkedIn profile is *[insert your goal, such as: get more clients / find a job / become a thought leader / sell my book]*.
>
> I want it to include:
> – My job titles or roles: *[insert roles]*
> – What I'm known for or best at: *[insert your strengths or results]*
> – A distinctive fact, quirk, or belief: *[insert something unique or intriguing about you]*
>
> Tone: *[insert tone — e.g., magnetic, confident, sharp]*
> Make it first-person implied (no "I" statements).
> Keep it under 220 characters. Do not use emojis.
> Give me 10 examples.
>
> Do you need any additional information from me?

SAMPLE HEADLINE SECTIONS

Use QR code in Chapter 4 or at the end of this book to view examples.

ACTION PLAN

☐ Click on the QR code and download the headline worksheet.

☐ Check out profile previews so you can see how few characters 40-50 really are.

☐ Review the examples above and then check out 5-10 headlines on profiles in your network. Ask yourself these questions:

- What is the purpose of their LinkedIn profile? What does this person want?

- What does this person do? What is their offer?

- How does this profile make me feel? Am I interested in learning more about them?

☐ Practice updating others' headlines. (Sometimes, it's easier to practice when it's not yours.)

☐ Update your own headline. Add icons and emojis as necessary. Follow the guidelines above.

CHAPTER 9

Intro

THE INTRO REFERS TO THE SECTION immediately under your profile picture. If you're looking at your profile, it's above "Suggested for you" and "Analytics." If you're looking at someone else's profile, it's above Highlights. See the sample profile in the book bonuses.

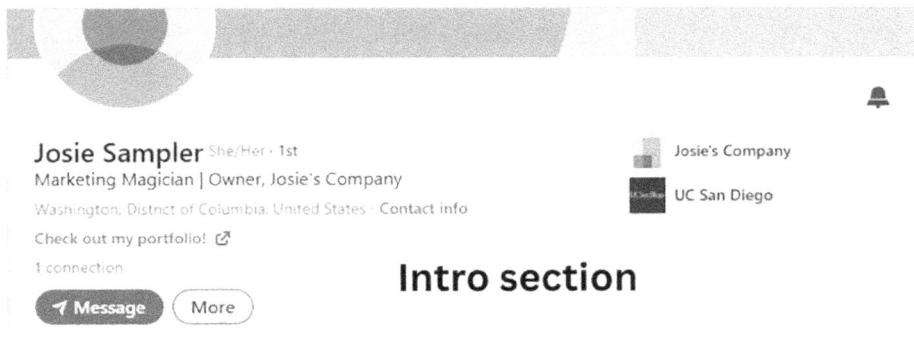

The purpose of the Intro section is to give folks who check out your profile a quick synopsis of what you offer, your experience, and how to get in touch with you. It is arguably one of the most important parts of your LinkedIn profile because it's where you're launching your charm offensive so people want to keep perusing your profile. This section is also where you start locking down your information security to help avoid being hacked or bombarded with emails and calls.

NOTE: What LinkedIn calls "Basic info" (your name and your headline) is part of the Intro section. However, your name and headline require more detailed consideration, so I gave them each their own chapter in this book.

CAREER PROFESSIONALS AND JOB SEEKERS

Everything in this section applies to you the same way it does business owners. Follow the guidelines below.

STRATEGY QUESTIONS

- Which position is most relevant to what I do now?
- Which education is most relevant to what I do now?
- What website do I have that can add the most impact in the different places in my Intro section?

This chapter is formatted differently from the others in order to cover each section within intro.

CURRENT POSITION

The default for this is the top-listed item in your experience section. If you prefer another option to show up here, you may need to rearrange your experience entries to put it on top. Only one position will show up at a time.

If you check the box "Show position in my intro," this position will show up to the right of your headline. This is why you need to have a company page, even for freelance work. If you don't, you'll end up with a DGS, and we know those are ugly.

INDUSTRY

This field is required. Pick the industry that most closely describes what you do. You need to pick from predetermined options, but they are generic enough that you should be able to find one that works for you.

This information doesn't actually show up in your Intro section. LinkedIn uses this to determine what they think will be of interest to you.

EDUCATION

Just like position, only one education will appear in the Intro section. It is designated as "required," but if you do not add anything to education, there's nothing to add.

If you want to share one of the schools you attended, then check "Show school in my intro." It will be the first one under your Experience section.

Do not check this box if you do not want this information featured in your intro. This field shows up immediately under the position field in your Intro section.

LOCATION

This is a required field, but that does not mean you should give precise information. From an online security standpoint, it's important to be as vague as possible.

- **Country/Region.** You must choose from a predefined list. In most cases, you should pick the country where you live and work, even if you work all over the world or virtually.

- **Postal code.** If you add your postal code, LinkedIn will tell everyone precisely where you live. Don't do that. If you want people to know which state, province, or area you're in, then pick a zip code from your closest large city. If you don't, leave this blank. If you leave this blank, LinkedIn will default to whichever country/region you added above.

- **City.** If you have no zip code entered, this field will not pop up. However, if you do, this is a required field. You can usually pick between the exact city/location by zip code or the closest metropolitan area.

CONTACT INFO

This is the pop-up box that shares your contact information. On a desktop it's found immediately under your headline at the end of your location. Look for a live link called "Contact info." On mobile, press the three little dots to the right of the Message button and scroll to "Contact Info."

This information fills out the contact info and pops up on your profile. To edit this, click on "Edit contact info."

- **Profile URL.** Yes, you can update this! You can remove all the extra code LinkedIn adds at the end and even change how your name appears. Use a URL that you can easily remember. Bonus if it's the same handle on other social media platforms. (This is rarely available, but always worth checking.)

- **Email.** The email address listed here will be the one you added when you signed up for LinkedIn. It's your login email. For this reason, do NOT make this email address public. (Unfortunately, LinkedIn does not give us the option of adding a separate email address for public consumption.) HIDE THIS. You can do this by going to Settings & Privacy > Visibility > Who can see or download your email address > Click on "Only visible to me" (first button).

- **Phone number.** Do not add a phone number. Definitely do not add your cell phone number. If you insist on having one here, use Google Voice or a service you do not use for authentication.

- **Phone type.** Irrelevant if you don't add a phone number.

- **Address.** Don't add this. Definitely don't add your home address. Yes, I know it's easy to find this information, but why make it easier? If you have a brick-and-mortar location, you can add the name of your business and street address here, as long as it's not your home address.

- **Birthday.** For security reasons, do not add your birthday to LinkedIn.

- **Website.** Any websites you list here (you can list multiple) will show up on the contact card. You can choose between company, blog, portfolio, etc. This is NOT the website listed under website in the general Intro section (see below).

  - Website URL/Website type. Update this for each website you want to add.

  - Click + Add website to add additional sites.

- **Instant messaging.** If you use or offer instant messaging, you can add the information here.

WEBSITE

This link will show up directly under your location. If you are tempted to add your URL to your headline, add it here instead. You can also add your link to your portfolio or schedule a call. The options are almost limitless!

CUSTOM BUTTON

At the time this book is being published, LinkedIn has decided to paywall this feature and add it Premium Business, Sales Navigator, and Recruiter Lite accounts. If you are paying for Premium Business, consider adding this button.

You will have the choice of None, Link, and Premium Custom Button. Only the last one will "follow you" all over LinkedIn, showing up directly under your headline, including when you post, comment, and in DMs.

If you don't have one of those accounts, this defaults to the link below your location (see above for the "Website" section).

ACTION PLAN

- ☐ Open the Intro section and fill out the information. It's one of the easiest things to fix on your profile.

- ☐ Check back regularly to make sure everything is updated.

- ☐ Do NOT include your email address, phone number, address, birthday, or anything else that can identify you personally.

CHAPTER 10

About

THE WILD THINGS THAT PEOPLE INCLUDE in their About section never cease to amaze me. I've seen it all, from skipping this section to the stories I shared in an earlier chapter to really long, detailed descriptions of their business and methods to every award they've ever won being listed.

I get it. We've been told that this section is like our cover letter for a job application. For that reason, we agonize over getting this About section right. I'm almost embarrassed at the number of HOURS I've spent writing this section myself, sometimes just to get my About section to under the maximum 2600 characters. (Do you have any idea how *long* that is? Very.) The irony is that no one wants to read a long-ass story or your methodology. And if we're honest, no one actually does. This is why we need to approach this section differently than we would if we were applying for a job.

The About section is your opportunity to invite someone into your world by telling them a story or making a compelling argument about why they should work with you. But as I reiterate in this book, it needs to be short and sweet.

Remember that despite the fact that the About section is at the top of your LinkedIn profile, it is often your *closing* argument, not your opening argument. You don't need to reiterate what can be easily found elsewhere in your amazing LinkedIn profile. Instead, use this section to make you interesting enough to call and share the problem you solve.

CAREER PROFESSIONALS AND JOB SEEKERS

Everything in this section applies to you the same way it does business owners. Follow the guidelines below, but keep in mind your potential employers and peers rather than your ideal clients.

STRATEGY QUESTIONS

- What's my story? Why or how did I get into my business?
- What is my competitive advantage?
- Is my ICP (ideal client profile) aligned with who I authentically am?
- What problem does my ICP want solved? Do they lack time? Money? Love? Something else?
- What are my values? What does my ICP value?
- What kind of format and information does my ICP need to get on a call with me or make a decision?
- What is my unique selling proposition?
- For career professionals: What do decision-makers and/or recruiters in my industry need to know to consider me for a position?

WHAT TO INCLUDE IN YOUR ABOUT SECTION

What you include in this section is dependent on your audience. See "How to format this section" below for ideas. However, the About section is also where you can include information that might not be included elsewhere on your LinkedIn profile but that people might search for.

Below are a few ideas of things you can include in your About section.

- **Your origin story.** If you have a cool or interesting story about how you started doing what you do, this is a great place to add it. However, you still need to make it short.
- **Your philosophy.** If there's something about the way you approach your work that makes you stand out, then you can add that here.
- **Your competitive advantage.** Tell us what makes you better than everyone else in your market.

- **Your ICP (ideal client profile) or ideal work environment.** Identify exactly who would be best served working with you.

- **Keywords and phrases.** At the bottom of your About section, you can add keywords and key phrases that may not be found elsewhere on your profile. These may not be directly relevant to your expertise but will put you in front of people who are looking in your industry overall. For example, if you are an architectural or building engineer, you might include architecture, mechanical engineering, building science, or sustainability.

- **Former names.** If you are known by another name, you can add it here if you do not want to add it to your Name section.

WHAT TO AVOID IN YOUR ABOUT SECTION

Unfortunately, the About section seems to be a popular repository for everything that people don't know where to put or somehow want front-and-center. All this does is make this section cluttered with too much information, so the important stuff doesn't get noticed.

Here are some things that do not need to be included in your About section.

- **Long dense paragraphs.** No one reads them. Save yourself time. Save your prospects time. Remember, this section gave you all this space because at one point, LinkedIn did not offer the opportunity to include live links. This is no longer the case, so keep it short.

- **A list of accolades.** This is why the Honors & Awards section exists. Instead, add a statement like, "For a list of honors and awards I've received, please see below."

- **A list of licenses and certifications.** Same as accolades, above.

- **Your life history.** Sorry, no one cares how you got to where you are. Unless you have an interesting or unique origin story, don't include this. (I think I'm still traumatized by that story I shared in an earlier chapter about that woman who detailed her childhood abuse in her About section.) If you are still compelled to add your life story, add this to your website instead.

- **A detailed recap of your business.** Again, no one reads these, especially now that LinkedIn offers multiple opportunities to add live links.

- **All of your offers.** You have plenty of opportunities on your profile to share your offers, including under services, featured, and experience. If you have one that you really want to highlight or is new, then that's fine, but do not add every offer you have.

- **Discordant information.** Know your audience. Do not include information or use a format that is jarring to your ICP.

HOW TO FORMAT THIS SECTION

If you think about this section as your most compelling closing argument, then it will be easier to decide what to include in this section. The key is to tailor this message to what your audience wants, but do it in a way that also reflects who you are and how you work. Authenticity is everything, so keep it real. If you are a laid-back informal person and you tend to use informal language, then do that.

Adapt the format of your message and what you include to meet the needs of your audience. For example, for an audience who wants a warm and welcoming coach, a fun, silly "letter" peppered with emojis could work well because that approach makes your ICP feel safe and good about working with you. They will like you, which is important to them.

Alternatively, if an audience is looking to hire an expert to save time and do an excellent job, they'd appreciate an acknowledgment that you will take care of everything for them and your level of excellence. You should also make sure that your message is short and to the point because they value getting things done quickly. In other words, don't waste their time. A bullet point list of the problems you solve would work.

Regardless, you want to keep to short sentences, short paragraphs, and lots of white space. The shorter the better because that makes it more likely someone will actually read it. Don't be afraid to use bullet points when appropriate.

AI/LLM PROMPT

Remember that prompts for the About section are also located in the book bonuses. Use the QR code to access them, including one that is a "Tell My Story" generator.

Help me write a first-person LinkedIn About section that tells my story while showing how I create impact.

My goal for my LinkedIn profile is *[insert your goal, such as: get more clients / find a job / become a thought leader / sell my book]*.

My audience is: *[insert who you want to reach]*
They care about: *[insert what they want or need]*
I want them to see that I: *[insert your unique value, approach, or superpower]*
Some key milestones or parts of my story include: *[insert 2-4 bullet points or moments]*

Tone: *[insert tone — e.g., honest, visionary, smart, no-fluff]*
Make the opening line bold and intriguing. Help me avoid clichés and make it sound like me.

What additional information do you need from me?

EXAMPLES AND ADDITIONAL AI/LLM PROMPTS FOR ABOUT SECTION

Use QR code in Chapter 4 or at the end of this book to view examples.

ACTION PLAN

☐ Write down your ICP's values and what they need from you to make a decision to hire you.

☐ Review your current About section.

☐ Move anything that you can add elsewhere to your profile or details that are readily available on your website.

☐ Delete anything superfluous to your LinkedIn ESD. Save it for later.

☐ Adapt your message to match the needs of your audience, but use language and tone that is authentic to you.

☐ Use a format that resonates with your ICP.

CHAPTER 11

Services

THE SERVICES SECTION is one of the newer additions to LinkedIn profiles, and few people use it, never mind using it to its full potential. To be fair, most of its benefits are available if you pay for Premium Business; however, there are still benefits to using it, even if you don't. The exception is if you only offer physical products for sale. If that's the case, ignore this section.

This section is unique in that it's the only section that is specifically geared toward sales and letting people know exactly what you do. For this reason, it makes sense to include it, *especially* if you're paying for Premium. Unfortunately, there isn't much flexibility in how you can format this, so it's important to take advantage of what you can leverage.

If you don't want to include this section, you don't have to. However, there are more benefits than not. Also, because there is no pretense in this section, your audience will know exactly what you offer, no external website necessary.

CAREER PROFESSIONALS AND JOB SEEKERS

If you are not offering consulting, coaching, or other services outside of your job, this section is not relevant for you.

Strategy questions

- Do I offer services?
- Are my services clearly defined?
- Which offers do I want to prioritize?

WHAT TO INCLUDE IN YOUR SERVICES SECTION

When you include this section on your LinkedIn profile, it shows up directly above "featured" and below "about." That means that once you include the Services section, and then add the services you offer, that list of services will show up as a bold list on your profile (or at least the first two lines do). If you have Premium Business, it will also show any media you upload (see below), which gives you another opportunity to reinforce branding and colors on your LinkedIn profile.

Note that the Services section does not offer much in terms of flexibility or space, so you will need to be concise and precise. Focus on the services you want to offer the most.

Additionally, take advantage of each section. I recommend using the three main sections (About, Services provided, and media) to get the biggest wow factor, even if you don't pay for Premium Business. It gives the quickest snapshot of what you offer, and done right, it is a great add-on to the rest of your profile.

WHAT TO AVOID IN YOUR SERVICES SECTION

As of the publication of this book there is a limit of 500 characters in this section (plus eight graphics). Because of the limited space, do not include anything personal. This is not the place to include your origin story or your why. Save that for your About section or a post.

Also, don't include offers that you really don't like, don't want to do, or can't do. Just because you're good at something does not mean that you have to offer it as a service.

Finally, unless you can remember to update later, don't include temporary offers.

HOW TO FORMAT ENTRIES

The Services section is not meant to be an engagement post, and there's no room for that. It is meant to be direct and factual. Below are how each element within services and how to approach them.

- **Services provided.** You may pick up to 10 items from a predetermined list. Unfortunately, this means that you cannot come up with your own descriptions, even if nothing is listed that accurately describes what you do. You will need to use your media for this purpose. Remember that you don't have to add 10 services, just use the descriptions that best generally describe what you offer.

  Note that these items show up in the order that you add them to your Services section; you cannot rearrange them after you add them. Therefore, explore the options, pick your top choices, put them in the order you want them, and *then* add them to services provided.

  I recommend adding the most significant ones first because LinkedIn limits visuals on your profile to the first two lines. If anyone is skimming your profile, they are most likely to see and register the first few services provided listed.

- **About.** You only have 500 characters for this section, considerably less than your personal About section and each entry in the experience section. Use this element to offer a short description of the kind of work you do. If you prefer, a bulleted list of who your services are for and what exactly you do work well here.

  I recommend writing this up in Google Docs or Word so that you can track how many characters you are using. Staying within the limits can be challenging, so this may take some effort.

  Finally, you can repeat what you have in your personal About section, but remember that you only have 500 characters, not the 2600 characters you get in your personal About section.

- **Media.** You may add up to eight forms of media (image, video, and link) to this section. However, you cannot add multi-page images or PDF files. On the plus side, you can rearrange the media once you've uploaded them. On the downside, you cannot change the thumbnail like you can in featured and the media in experience entries, so you want to make sure that the media is sized correctly so that it's legible.

If you have Premium Business, these will show up on your LinkedIn profile immediately above the list of services you picked. Depending on how many you have, they will show up as a carousel. It's another great opportunity to reinforce your branding and colors, grabbing your audience's attention. Even if you're not paying for Premium Business, this will still be effective.

The most effective way to use this section is by creating slides that outline what you want your audience to know. Save them as png or jpg/jpeg files, since LinkedIn limits which types of files you can add here. Here's a sample list of slides to include, in the order that makes the most sense for most of us.

- Cover slide.

- Area of expertise or general offerings. You can also add general ICP information, but detailed ICP and examples can be added to last slide.

- Service(s) + fee (one slide for each service), OR

- Services you offer.

- Packages or fees, or how you price your fees. You can also say something like, "Start at..."

- Details on ICP, including examples of ICP.

- Testimonials or links to testimonials.

■ **Other elements.** Fill out work location and pricing.

■ **Messages.** Say yes to "messages" if you want anyone to be able to reach out to you. Unfortunately, this requires you to have an open profile, which means you're willing to accept messages from anyone on LinkedIn. In general, that seems to invite a lot more unsolicited sales pitches, but if you don't mind that, you should include it.

■ **Reviews visibility.** This is the closest that LinkedIn has to a review scale for your products and services. However, unlike the Recommendations section, you do not get to review what someone says before it posts. Additionally, it has a star rating, and while reviewers can update their reviews, they cannot change their star rating. Finally, you can invite up to 20 people to leave you a review. If you choose to include this element, make sure you're very careful about whom you're inviting to leave you a review.

AI/LLM PROMPT

This prompt is for the About section within the Services section. To access prompts for media graphics (see above), use the QR code.

Help me write a compelling LinkedIn Services section.

My goal for my LinkedIn profile is *[insert your goal, such as: get more clients / become a thought leader / sell my book].*

I offer: *[insert services — consulting, speaking, coaching, etc.]*

I work with: *[insert types of clients or industries]*

I want potential clients to know: *[insert any differentiators, results, or your approach]*

Write in first-person and keep it clear, concise, confident, and results-oriented.

Limit to 500 characters.

Use bullet points. *(← This is optional.)*

SAMPLE SERVICES SECTIONS

Use QR code in Chapter 4 or at the end of this book to view examples.

ACTION PLAN

☐ If you haven't already, add the Services section to your profile.

☐ Review the services provided options, and pick out the ones that make the most sense for what you do. You may want to write them down. They are not likely to exactly match what you do.

☐ Reorder them. Remember to put the most significant first.

☐ Add them to services provided in the order in which you want them to appear.

☐ Add your About section. Remember that this is specific to your services, not your personal story or perspective. It is also incredibly short (only 500 characters). And yes, using "&" and "b/c" to save space is okay here.

☐ Create slides for your media. Each slide should be saved as png or jpg/jpeg and be saved separately. For better impact, remember to be consistent with your branding and colors.

☐ You can also add links or videos here. If you do, remember that you cannot change the thumbnail, so be sure that the first frame looks exactly how you want it to look.

CHAPTER 12

Featured

IF YOUR HEADLINE IS THE FIRST TEASER, and your banner is your promise, the Featured section of your LinkedIn profile is the enticement where your audience can get to know more about you and what you do. This is where you get to invite people into your world using deliberately curated content and color.

The Featured section is traditionally the place where you'd pin the posts you wrote about accolades you received, articles written by and about you, and maybe events coming up. However, this section is also a great opportunity to direct your audience to what you want them to consider. It's the first place you get to introduce them to your offers, your personality, and how to engage with you, especially if you're not paying for Premium Business.

Featured is the one section that requires regular updates unless you are using static links (websites, links to calendar scheduler, etc.).

CAREER PROFESSIONALS AND JOB SEEKERS

Everything in this section applies to you similarly to the way it does founders and business owners. Follow guidelines below, but keep in mind your peers, potential employers, or recruiters rather than your ideal clients. The Featured section is an important part of your personal branding.

STRATEGY QUESTIONS

■ Which of my branding colors pops? (Career professionals and job seekers should also consider applying branding colors.)

■ What do I want my audience to know about me or my business that's not immediately obvious or doesn't require a deep dive into my portfolio?

■ What information can I share that will tip my audience from "exploring" to "scheduling a call"?

■ For career professionals: Which posts, information, portfolios, or engagements can I share that demonstrates my expertise to my peers and potential employers?

WHAT TO INCLUDE IN YOUR FEATURED SECTION

There are many options to include in this section, and what you choose depends on how you are leveraging your LinkedIn profile. But first, let's talk about what you can include.

LinkedIn allows you to add links, posts, your LinkedIn newsletter, articles you've written and posted on LinkedIn, documents, and photos. So, anything that fits these parameters can be included here.

In addition to native LinkedIn options, here are some other ideas:

■ Links to your website, landing page, etc.

■ Link to your portfolio

■ Link to your calendar (to schedule appointments)

■ Pitch deck (can also be deck of offers)

■ Link to your podcast

■ Links to testimonials

■ Link to YouTube video of a speech

■ Posts where you are featured

The hardest part here is deciding what to include. It's easy to add everything, but since LinkedIn only shows the first three entries on a desktop (only the first one on the app), it is worth deliberately curating what is included, including the order of the entries.

To be most impactful, be sure to leverage your branding and colors. (See below for a detailed explanation.)

WHAT TO AVOID IN YOUR FEATURED SECTION

There isn't much to avoid including in this section. If it works to support your overall LinkedIn strategy, it's worth including. However, for the sake of clarity, I've included a short list of what not include:

- Old posts
- Irrelevant posts
- Dead links
- Events that have already passed
- Random posts that you think are interesting but don't add to your overall narrative or strategy

If it doesn't directly help you reach the goal of your LinkedIn profile, don't include it.

HOW TO APPROACH YOUR FEATURED SECTION

Earlier in this chapter, I noted that what you include in this section is dictated by the goal you've set for your LinkedIn profile. In short, you want to include links that lead people to want to work with you or follow you. Below are some suggestions based on your possible goals:

- **Thought leader.** This is not a client-focused profile, so links to posts and articles that you wrote or where you're quoted are useful here. You can also include links to your blog or podcast, photos of you speaking, accolades, and your one sheet or an invitation to book you to speak.

- **Creative (freelancer or anyone with a portfolio).** This is a client-seeking profile, and clients tend to hire you for projects. Include your portfolio, landing page, or deck of offers (if you have set prices or descriptions), testimonials, or a recent award you won. You can also include a link to your calendar.

- **Done-for-You (DFY) service provider.** This is a client-seeking profile, and clients hire you to do something for them in a DFY manner, like build a website or fix their IT. Include your landing page or deck of offers, portfolio of your work (if appropriate), your calendar link, testimonials, or videos that showcase your expertise.

- **Service provider (consultant, coach, etc.).** This is a client-seeking profile, and you tend to work with clients directly to accomplish a goal. Include your calendar link, your landing page, links to your blog or podcast, links to your lead magnet, your landing page, your offer deck, or links to courses you created and are selling.

- **Startup seeking funding.** You are in development and are actively seeking funding. You may not want to include your whole pitch deck, but you can include the link to your website, links, or a document that talks about what you're doing in general terms and how to reach you. To prove your mettle in your industry, this is a great place to feature articles you've written or your blog, any videos you may have created to share your vision, and opportunities you've had to pitch or present.

- **Product (physical product, from consumer packaged goods to equipment).** You may not sell your product directly through LinkedIn, but you can still find clients or contacts here. Include links to your website or landing pages, use case studies you may have on your website (can be repeated below under Projects section), and third-party validation.

Remember, the key here is to include entries that build the case someone needs to hire or follow you. This is not meant to take the place of the sales cycle (although that's possible), but having everything readily available for your prospects to review will definitely help. And once they get on a call with you, they'll be ready to buy.

USING COLOR TO AMPLIFY YOUR FEATURED SECTION

In the chapter called *Strategy*, I explain how color can amplify your profile. The Featured section is a great place to do this. Remember, the eye is attracted to color, so anything colorful will stand out since your LinkedIn profile is otherwise black and white.

However, to bring in the wow factor, be sure your chosen color is uniform and vibrant. In the Featured section, this looks like each thumbnail uniform in size, and the same color or color palette across each entry. Reminder: you can change the thumbnail, so you don't have to change the links or articles.

As far as the best color goes, it doesn't have to be your primary branding color or hot pink, but the color should be enough to capture the attention of your audience when they are glancing at your LinkedIn profile. That generally leaves out darker, more muted colors, like forest green or brown, as the primary color.

I get this seems like overkill, but when profiles use color to make their Featured section entries look uniform, they get more engagement and schedule more calls. This is true even when each thumbnail has the exact same color and picture, with only the words changing.

DESIGNING YOUR FEATURED SECTION

You've picked out what to include in your Featured section, and you've decided on a vibrant color that will stand out when someone skims your profile. The next two things to do are to decide in what order your entries should go and to design the thumbnails for each entry to maintain that uniformity.

I'd recommend starting with what people want to know first. For some, it makes sense to start with their offers, then their portfolio, and then other items. Others might start with the lead magnet or links to their podcast. The question to ask yourself is, what is the journey I want to take my audience on? Following that often works well.

A few notes: The title (required) will appear under your entry, and a long title will take up two lines. Try to keep it short. You do not need a description. This takes up space, so it will change the size of your thumbnail. Also, you can rearrange entries after you've added them.

The next thing to consider is how many entries to include. If you only have one entry, the thumbnail for that entry will take up the whole space, widthwise. The maximum it'll show is three entries, and then your audience must click on the arrow to access the others. This is why it's so important to get the order of the first ones right and why you don't want a never-ending list of entries. This is another case of more is not necessarily better.

To make that uniformity really pop, design a thumbnail of the size and design that can be used across all entries. You will need to add the media (links, documents, .jpeg, etc.) first and save it. Then, go back and change the thumbnail for each entry. Some folks will use the exact same thumbnail, only changing the words to identify the purpose for each entry. Others will use the same color and design themes but change it up according to the purpose of each entry.

AI/LLM PROMPT

Edit this prompt with your information.

> Help me decide what to include in my LinkedIn Featured section.
>
> My goal for my LinkedIn profile is *[insert your goal, such as: get more clients / become a thought leader / find a job / sell my book].*
>
> I want to showcase: *[insert types of content — videos, articles, interviews, client wins, programs, etc.]*
>
> My goal is to: *[insert goal — e.g., build credibility, generate leads, establish authority]*
>
> Give me suggestions for 3-5 things I could feature, including what the title or description should say to make people click.

SAMPLE FEATURED SECTIONS

Use QR code in Chapter 4 or at the end of this book to view examples.

ACTION PLAN

☐ Remove any old or irrelevant items currently in your Featured section.

☐ Decide what you'll include in the Featured section.

☐ Verify any links for any items you are keeping.

☐ Add new entries. If possible, keep it to fewer than seven. (Fewer is better.)

☐ Reorder entries. The first one will show up farthest left.

☐ Pick a vibrant brand color to use on your thumbnails.

☐ Design thumbnail(s). Keep size uniform.

☐ Change thumbnails for each entry. Remember to save the entry before changing the thumbnail.

☐ Re-verify all media, including any links.

CHAPTER 13

Experience

WE ARE AT THE PART OF YOUR LINKEDIN PROFILE that people tend to think of as "the resume" portion. However, if you are a founder or business owner, you will approach this quite differently than career professionals and job seekers.

Some folks add every job they've ever had, whether it was employment, internship, freelance work, collaboration, or advisor. The result is an incredibly long list of entries, many of which are similar or irrelevant. This really long list is one of the reasons I recommend putting advisory clients under the Projects or Volunteering section.

Unlike how career professionals and job seekers use this section, experience is not best used to feature a litany of achievements in your business. Instead, use your experience description to feature the mission of each business or the transformation that your ICP (ideal client profile) will experience. Your entries are not little sales pages where you list every offer or a resume of the litany of tasks for which you are responsible. Instead, add your short elevator pitch about your business.

If you are both currently employed *and* own a business, then this could be a hybrid. You have options. If you're using your LinkedIn profile primarily for your business and not your job, then limit the content you add under your Experience section. You can add that you are currently employed at ACME Company, but you'll treat the description similar to below for businesses you've founded, plus a one sentence description to explain your job and tasks if it's not obvious. Oftentimes, it makes more sense to add detailed information (like reaching your KPIs) to your LinkedIn emotional support document, thus keeping the details or the lengthy list of successes off LinkedIn. When you are looking for new employment, you can add it again. The other option is to not include your job at all.

CAREER PROFESSIONALS AND JOB SEEKERS

If you are not using your LinkedIn profile as a hybrid (job and side hustle), then your focus should be on your achievements in your job. One thing remains the same: keep your lists short and descriptive. Also, limit your achievements to 3–5 bullet points. Any more than that, it won't be read. To supplement your job search, have a resume available.

Note that LinkedIn is actively implementing AI tools to quickly sift through job applicants. At the time I am writing this, how those tools are fully implemented and what they look for are still not clear. Therefore, your goal is to be interesting to the humans who are looking for candidates, especially for higher-level jobs. And pay attention to how AI will be used for job searches.

STRATEGY QUESTIONS

- What is the main purpose of my LinkedIn profile?
- If I am employed (not freelance), then am I okay with featuring my business as my primary focus on my LinkedIn profile?
- Which professional experiences have I had that best showcases my expertise?
- What do I need to say for someone to hire me? What are they thinking?

WHAT TO INCLUDE IN YOUR EXPERIENCE SECTION

Remember your goal for your LinkedIn profile as you update this section. It is tempting to add all the tasks for which you are responsible and everything you've accomplished. Resist!! No one reads those long, detailed entries, so make what you want to say count.

Besides, LinkedIn only shows the first two lines of each experience, so to maximize impact, you need to make those two lines count.

- **Only include relevant work.** No one cares that you used to work at Best Buy or a flower shop or data entry when you were young. Unless it's relevant or you are young and need to show a consistent work pattern, save it in your ESD and delete the entries.

- **Only include the last 10–20 years.** Things are changing so rapidly in the workforce that including work you did more than this frame dates you rather than adding to your story. The exceptions are if that old work is relevant or significant to what you're doing now, or you've owned your company for longer than that time.

- **Signal that you own or founded the company.** Give yourself credit! Add "Founder" or "Owner" to your job title. Plus people like knowing that you are the founder or boss, and not just a "Global Change Consultant."

- **Add description of your company and the transformation you provide.** But make it short and sweet. Remember, they will only see the first two lines when they skim your profile. Please don't leave this blank because most of the time, the name of your business does not explain what you do.

  Career professionals and job seekers can add one or two sentences that describe your job, if it isn't obvious by the job title or isn't industry standard. Additionally, you may add 3-5 bullet points of your greatest achievements.

- **Use an active company page.** You want to avoid the DGB as much as you can, so if you have a business, then set up a company page on LinkedIn, even if it's freelancing or your old company is closed. It's free and does not take much time to do.

  Career professionals and job seekers should make sure that their job is connected to an active company page as well. Note that sometimes the company page isn't titled exactly as you know it, so look it up on LinkedIn first, and then use that wording.

- **Add media with links.** One of the cool things about LinkedIn is the ability to add media, including graphics and links, to each entry in your Experience section. Take advantage of this to reinforce branding and share additional information. See below for how to do this.

WHAT TO AVOID IN YOUR EXPERIENCE SECTION

Limiting anything not absolutely necessary is really hard to do. The goal is to include the bare minimum with maximum effect, which is even more important now that LinkedIn only shows the first two lines of your Experience section entries (and most other sections). So if you find yourself wanting to include anything listed below, rethink it.

- **Your job responsibilities.** If you're a founder or business owner, it goes without saying that you are responsible for marketing, sales, and managing finances. That is not helpful information, so skip it.

  Career professionals and job seekers can add a sentence or two, but do not add every single thing you do.

- **Everything your company does and every offer you have.** Again, no one reads that much text. Instead, include it in the following sections: Services, Featured, About (very short version), and even your company page. You can also use media to send people to your website or social media, or to explain your offers. But skip all the words.

- **Case studies and success stories.** Instead, use the Projects section. You can state something like, "For case studies, see Projects below."

  Career professionals should also use the Projects section liberally.

- **Employment type.** LinkedIn no longer requires you to identify your work as part-time, full-time, self-employed, etc. In many cases, it's not worth including. The exception would be if you do freelance work, but even then it's not necessary. Why eliminate this? From a founder's or business owner's perspective, this is irrelevant information. Sometimes we work a lot in our business, sometimes we don't work at all in it, sometimes we jump between projects. Also, they are often misleading. And finally, it's mostly women who tend to self-identify as self-employed, even when they employ others. (I even wrote an article for *Fast Company* about this.)

  Career professionals and job seekers usually benefit from adding employment type.

- **No description.** That's almost as bad as too much information because you haven't explained what you do and are requiring people to figure it out or click off your profile. Don't do that. Add a very short description.

  Career professionals and job seekers should confirm that the experience is linked to an active company page (no dreaded gray box).

- **Very short engagements.** Sometimes you took part in a day, weekend, or several weeks event. They may be job related, but not always. For students or recent graduates, this could be a 2-day Model UN forum or case competition. These are often best listed under the experience entry you worked when it happened or under the Projects section.

- **Every internship you've ever had.** I had to rethink my stance on this when I recently came across a student's profile who listed 16 internships and short engagements. They were way too young to have that much in their Experience section. If they are shorter than a couple weeks or not directly related to your chosen career field, add them to your Projects section. If you only have a couple, it's okay to leave them in your Experience section.

- **Advisory positions.** This is a stylistic opinion, but too many entries in the Experience section can be off-putting and distracting, so they don't get read because there's too much. Instead, list (bullet point) the companies you've advised under your company, and list them in your Projects section instead. You can use your company's Experience section entry to point folks to the Projects section. Bonus: Under the Projects section, you can tag the founder you advised.

- **Month.** This one is optional, but with the older entries, you don't need to add the month. You have the option of adding only the year (which is required). The way to do this is by picking the "--" right above "January." There's no problem adding the month if you want, but it's just not necessary. If your entry is old or your business is no longer in business, skip the month.

HOW TO FORMAT ENTRIES

Adding an entry is simple, but there are a few things to note as you add or edit your entries.

■ **Title.** You have 100 characters to give your job title. Be descriptive AND add "Founder," "Owner," or something that designates this as YOUR business. Otherwise, it sounds like it belongs to someone else and you're not working for you.

Career professionals and job seekers should add their official title, including the department, if relevant.

■ **Employment type.** See above. It's important.

■ **Company name.** If you haven't already, create your company page first. Then you can add the company name, and it'll pull up the company page. If you've already added your company to your Experience section, create a company page anyway and then add change your company name or add a new entry (and delete the old one).

NOTE: If you've done freelance work, then create a company page for your freelance work.

■ **Location.** Most of the time, leave this blank, especially if you mostly work virtually. If you want to include a location, use a zip code that is NOT yours, but rather a local large city. (This is a security issue.)

■ **Location type.** Not required, and in most cases, don't use it unless you have a physical location that is NOT your home.

■ **Dates.** You don't need month and year, but if it's only a few years old, then include month.

■ **Description.** LinkedIn only shows the first two lines, so make them count. Resist the temptation to include everything! (See above.) Your description should be very short and direct. Your "I help" statement can be used here, but it's usually better to use that to inspire the description. You can add a bullet point list of services, but you can also add those on your company page, Services section, and in your media.

Career professionals and job seekers should include no more than 3-5 bullet points of key achievements.

- **Skills.** Add the skills you have listed in the Skills section. Don't add everything you've ever done. See the *Skills* chapter for more detail.

- **Media.** This is one of the best features of this section because each entry can have its own graphics. You can add PNG, JPEG, and website links here. It's a great opportunity to add color and live links. (See *Strategy* chapter for full explanation.) Here are some ideas on how to use your media section:

  - Links to your other social media profiles (YouTube, TikTok, Facebook, Instagram, Pinterest, etc.).

  - Link to your portfolio

  - Link to your website

  - Links to courses you offer

  - Offers deck or pitch deck

Graphics sizes are standard but subject to change. Check the QR code in this book for the most recent sizes. Be sure to use colors and themes that reflect back to your own branding.

IMPORTANT NOTE: You can change the cover graphic that shows up for a link to a website or social media page. However, you MUST save the link first, and then go back and change the cover graphic by clicking on the pencil. If you do them both at the same time, you may lose the link.

AI/LLM PROMPT

There are two prompts below, depending on whether the entry is for your business or a business you founded, or whether the entry is for job seeking.

Remember to review each entry to make sure it says what you want it to say and how you want to say it. If it doesn't or if it focuses on something you do not consider relevant or important, you can ask your AI/LLM to redo it, but explain the issue.

Founder:

Help me write a compelling LinkedIn Experience section for my role as a founder or business owner.

My goal for my LinkedIn profile is *[insert your goal, such as: get more clients / become a thought leader / find a job / sell my book]*.

I want the first two lines to:
– Give a clear summary of what the business does
– Convey its purpose, vision, or unique positioning
– Mention one major result, impact, or achievement

Here are the details:
Role/title: *[insert your role — e.g., Founder & CEO]*
Business name: *[insert company name]*
Years active: *[insert start–end or "present"]*
What the business does: *[insert short summary — audience + solution]*
Core purpose or philosophy: *[insert why this business exists]*
Key wins or milestones: *[insert 2–4 — revenue, reach, awards, pivots, impact]*
Your role in making it all work: *[insert a few bullet points]*

Tone: *[describe tone, ex: Confident, clear, and founder-forward. Not overly polished or jargon-heavy.]*
Write in first-person. Avoid corporate-speak, I want it to sound human and real.

What additional information do you need from me?

Job-seeking professional:

Help me write a strong LinkedIn Experience section for a job-seeking professional.

My goal for my LinkedIn profile is *[insert your goal, such as: get more clients / become a thought leader / find a job / sell my book]*.

I want the first two lines to:
– State the purpose or function of the role
– Highlight a specific result or unique contribution I made

Here are the details:
Job title: *[insert title]*
Company: *[insert company name]*
Years worked: *[insert dates]*
Role summary: *[insert what this role focused on]*
Big wins: *[insert 2–4 examples of success, metrics, initiatives, or challenges overcome]*
Unique contribution: *[insert what you did differently or better than most]*

Tone: *[describe tone, ex: Clear, confident, results-driven, not robotic.]*
Write in first-person.
Focus on outcomes, not just responsibilities.

What additional information do you need from me?

SAMPLE EXPERIENCE SECTION ENTRIES

To view examples and additional AI/LLM prompts, use QR code in Chapter 4 or at the end of this book.

ACTION PLAN

☐ Open your ESD (LinkedIn emotional support document) because you're probably going to need it.

☐ Delete any jobs that are old (more than 10-20 years old), irrelevant to your current work, or entry level. Only keep them if they add credibility, but remember that older entries will also age you, which can be a problem once you're over 40 or 50 years old.

☐ Create a company page for any businesses you've owned that do not have one

☐ Go through each entry and be sure to adjust the following:
  - Your title
  - Company name matches a company page
  - Remove location to NOT be based on your postal code
  - Rewrite description to be short and impactful.

☐ Add relevant media (with branding) to each entry.

☐ Reorder entries to most relevant first. That's the one that will show up at the top, under your banner.

CHAPTER 14

Education

SOMETIMES I THINK THE ONLY PURPOSE of the Experience section is for people from my alma maters to network with me to sell me something or to get me to hire them. However, it is also a point of mutual connection when you're networking, so it's useful to get it right. And unlike other sections of your LinkedIn profile, it's pretty easy to do.

Additionally, if you have formal post-secondary education, such as college, university, or trade school, your degrees can provide you with additional validation and affirmation that you are qualified to do the things you say you can do.

CAREER PROFESSIONALS AND JOB SEEKERS

Everything in this section applies to you the same way it does business owners.

STRATEGY QUESTION

- What post secondary education do I have that I can leverage to support my expertise or that is relevant to my current field?

- Which education experiences do I have that are irrelevant or may undermine my professional credentials?

WHAT TO DO IF YOU DON'T HAVE A COLLEGE DEGREE OR OTHER TECHNICAL EDUCATION

One of the smartest people I've ever known is a man who didn't even finish high school. He's also one of the most successful business people I know. Your education or lack thereof does not define you. There is no shame in not having a college degree, especially when you're a business owner or have a set of desirable skills.

The truth is that in many cases, the longer it's been since you went to college, the less relevant it is where you got your degree, especially when you're in a profession that requires continuing education.

However, I'd be remiss in suggesting that where you went to university and what degrees you have don't play a role in certain industries. The best way to avoid this issue is by simply not including this section on your LinkedIn profile at all. Adding your high school (especially with that dreaded gray box) will highlight the fact that you did not receive formal education after high school. It's no one's damn business and it's a cybersecurity concern (since a common security question is "What was your high school mascot?") so just skip this section.

WHAT TO INCLUDE IN YOUR EXPERIENCE SECTION

- **College and university experience.** Include any college-level degree, or the progress you are making toward a college degree. It is not necessary to include that one summer class you took at your local community college so that you didn't have to take it during the regular school year.

- **Trade school and other post-secondary formal training.** If you completed other formal education that isn't a college degree but is important to your work, such as massage therapy school or aesthetician school, then this can also be added here.

  If you attended a trade school that is not relevant to your work, or for which you have not kept up the required CEUs, then it's sometimes better to remove them from your profile. However, like everything else related to your profile, the choice is yours.

WHAT AVOID IN YOUR EXPERIENCE SECTION

■ **Your high school.** Do not include your high school, unless there is a compelling reason to do so. I have yet to see a compelling reason that might make it relevant, but perhaps you went to an independent (private) school that is useful for networking. In that case, it makes sense to add, but only if that school has a LinkedIn company page and a substantial number of alumni have already identified it as their alma mater. If it doesn't, then it won't be useful for networking, since it's through your alma mater's company page that LinkedIn connects you.

■ **Dates (depending on your age).** Ageism continues to be a problem, and with it the assumption that if you're over a certain age, your skills are no longer relevant. For this reason, if you graduated more than 20 years ago, I strongly recommend that you do not include the dates you attended your schools or when you received your trade training completion. Additionally, listing attendance dates gives scammers additional information that they can use to steal your identity or run a scam on you.

■ **Licenses or certifications.** These do not belong in this section (including those handed out at the end of a weekend seminar), since LinkedIn offers another section where you can include this. It is called Licenses & Certifications.

LINK TO THE COMPANY PAGES

Whatever you do, try to make sure your education matches back to a company page so that the logo shows up, instead of the DGB (dreaded gray box).

If there is no company page with the name you entered, do a search on LinkedIn to see if the name has changed or isn't exactly what you call it. This happens more often than you might expect. Be sure to use the exact name so that the favicon shows up in the DGB.

WHAT IF THERE IS NO COMPANY PAGE?

If there is no company page, look for the "parent" company page. For example, if you went to the School of Education at Indiana State University, but it didn't have its own LinkedIn page, then you'd use the Indiana State University's LinkedIn page.

Alternatively, if there is no "parent" organization, you can add the website under the media section of each education.

If the school is closed and the website no longer exists, simply note this in the comments.

BE PRECISE

It is very easy to verify your education, especially by someone who is an alumnus of the school you claim. If you're caught lying about that, then it's easy to dismiss everything else you claim to have accomplished.

If you think that I'm exaggerating, note this: I recently read a story of a man who lied about his education credentials. He never finished the degree he claimed he had. So 20 years into his professional career, he was fired and his credibility was shot. He's not likely to find a job anytime soon in his industry.

It's not worth the lie.

Therefore, if you took a class or finished a program at Harvard Extension School, then do not claim Harvard University as your alma mater. (There is definitely a LinkedIn page for Harvard Extension School.) The same goes for an executive MBA or similar program at nearly any university, again, unless they don't have a page.

The exception would be if a night or global campus program identifies itself as an extension of the standard program. In that case, it makes sense to use the general name of the standard program.

The best rule of thumb here is to use the school that's listed on your degree.

FILLING IN THE REST OF THE EDUCATION DESCRIPTION

The final sections of each education entry are grade, activities, and societies, and description. The first two are more relevant to newer graduates, so unless you graduated valedictorian or salutatorian or with some distinguished honor, skip the grade. The same goes for activities and societies, unless it's relevant to your work. Fraternities and sororities will be listed under the Organizations section of your profile. Sorry, but no one cares that you founded the Underwater Basket Weaving Club at your undergraduate school.

Description is particularly useful for trades or programs that do not have obvious outcomes. For example, if you are a massage therapist, it might make sense to explain what type of massage therapy you learned, since there are over two dozen types.

ACTION PLAN

☐ Delete this section if you do not have a college degree or trade school completion.

☐ Do not add your high school here, unless there is a compelling reason to add it. (This is unusual.)

☐ Use the precise name of your alma mater so that your information can be properly verified.

☐ If your alma mater is not listed on LinkedIn, verify its name hasn't changed; or

☐ If your alma mater is not listed on LinkedIn, you can add the URL under the media section of your education entry. (Scroll to bottom.)

☐ Remove all dates if you completed your education more than 20 years ago, or even more recently.

☐ In most cases, skip the grade and activities and societies sections.

☐ Description is useful for trades to explain what you studied.

CHAPTER 15

Licenses & Certifications

THE PURPOSE OF THIS SECTION is to showcase that you've met the requirements of a third-party entity that now considers you an expert in that area. The biggest difference is that licenses are required by the government, like needing a license to practice medicine, give financial advice, or call yourself an architect. Certifications, on the other hand, are validations that you've met certain standards or requirements established by a private organization, which may be for-profit or not-for-profit.

Note that the value of a certification is in the quality of the organization that created it, and it's pretty easy to create a certification. I know this because I've created several for a company I worked for years ago. The good news is that because that company taught the content well, the folks who went through the certification process were seen as the best. However, a competing organization did the same, and their folks were not as successful on the topic, so their certification tended to weigh down the value and quality of their attendees.

CAREER PROFESSIONALS AND JOB SEEKERS

Everything in this section applies to you the same way it does founders and business owners. Follow the guidelines below, but keep in mind your potential employers rather than your ideal clients.

STRATEGY QUESTIONS

■ What licenses do I have that are current and that my ideal clients might find helpful?

■ Which certifications do I have that add validation to my offers?

WHEN TO INCLUDE YOUR LICENSES

First—because this question will come up—let me state that unless you're a truck driver who specializes in carrying a special kind of cargo, this section does not refer to a driver's license. It's a professional license.

TIP: If you *did* add your driver's license to this section, please stop reading now and go immediately to your profile and delete it. It's a security issue.

In some industries, your license is everything and so whether to share the information on LinkedIn could depend on whether and where you practice your profession. Being able to practice law in multiple jurisdictions, for example, would make you more valuable to certain clients or employers.

On the other hand, if you decide to give up architecture to do photography instead, then you may not need or want to include the details on your architecture license. If you decide to return to architecture, you can always add it later.

Note that licenses generally have an expiration date, and to maintain them, you need to submit proof of continuing education.

WHEN TO INCLUDE YOUR CERTIFICATIONS

The problem with certifications is also the thing that makes them generally easy to acquire. There is no standard for completion or confirmation that proves you know your stuff. Often they are simple, short webinars that don't even have a testing component (or have an easy testing component).

The value of a certification is fully rooted in the organization that issues the certification.

I once worked with someone whose work was clearly AI-written, and when I approached them on how to prime ChatGPT so that their work didn't sound like AI, I was informed that they'd taken "all the [AI] certifications available and passed each one." At the time, that included at least seven different certification programs. And yet, they didn't know how to prime ChatGPT.

Another LinkedIn profile I perused boasted 20+ certifications. A student who asked me to view their profile had over 60! This sounded impressive until I realized that most were from LinkedIn and Hubspot, and some were ridiculously simple and irrelevant to their professed field of expertise.

On the other hand, when I see that someone was certified by the International Coaching Federation, I know that to pass that, they've had to undergo hundreds of hours of training. If you agree with their methodologies, an ICF certification is impressive.

Also, some fields depend heavily on specific certifications, such as the financial industry and IT side of cybersecurity. However, those certifications will likely be associated with the specific company pages of the parent organizations.

Note that some certifications have expiration dates, so make sure the ones you share are current.

MATCH WITH ORGANIZATION'S COMPANY PAGE

Most, if not all, legitimate organizations that offer certifications will have a company page on LinkedIn. If it does not come up when you type in the name, then search for it on LinkedIn to make sure that the name hasn't changed. (This happens more often than you might think.) You *really* want to ensure the organization is legit, and the company page does this. A DGB decreases the value of that certification because what legitimate organization that offers certifications or licensing doesn't have a company page on LinkedIn today?

WHEN TO SKIP THIS SECTION

For many of us, this section isn't particularly relevant and won't make or break a deal. What I mean is that your ICP's decision to hire you will not depend on whether or not you have a particular certification. In many cases, you'll derive more benefit from showing off your skills through projects, your portfolio, or testimonials.

However, it also isn't likely to hurt to include your certifications, as long as they are quality and relevant certifications. Don't waste space on superfluous certifications.

WHAT TO AVOID IN YOUR LICENSES & CERTIFICATIONS SECTION

Do not include expired or irrelevant certifications unless there's a compelling reason to do so.

USING THIS SECTION FOR ADVISORY POSITIONS

I've seen some folks use this section for advisory positions. This works because you can easily tie it to the company's company page. However, I would recommend that you use the Projects section instead. I go into more detail in the *Projects* chapter of this book.

ACTION PLAN

☐ Collect all your licenses and certifications.

☐ Determine which are relevant to your ICP.

☐ Confirm they are up to date.

☐ Add relevant and current licenses and certifications to your LinkedIn profile.

☐ Be sure that all tie back to a company page so you don't have any dreaded gray boxes.

CHAPTER 16

Projects

AS I WAS WRITING THIS BOOK, a friend of mine told me that she saw LinkedIn as "kind of a light resume." If you've read the starting chapters in this book, you know that I adamantly disagree with this assessment. The Projects section is one of the biggest reasons why.

Once I explained to my friend about how she could use the Projects section to feature the work she's done, she was blown away. She'd been trying to figure out how to showcase the projects she's overseen so that she could demonstrate how effective she is at what she does.

Showing off is the whole point of this section.

CAREER PROFESSIONALS AND JOB SEEKERS

Everything in this section applies to you the same way it does founders and business owners. Follow the guidelines below, but keep in mind your potential employers rather than your ideal clients.

STRATEGY QUESTIONS

- What projects have I worked on that showcases my talents and expertise?
- Are these projects public knowledge or can be discussed without harming the client's IP or confidentiality?
- Which clients have I advised or worked with that warrant more than a footnote in my Experience section?

WHAT TO INCLUDE IN YOUR PROJECTS SECTION

What to include depends on several factors, including the type of work you do, if the projects you worked on were for clients (or at work), and what can be added here to supplement or showcase other sections of your LinkedIn profile.

Additionally, because the Projects section allows media (including websites), it offers an opportunity to feature topics that aren't highlighted elsewhere on your profile, like advisory positions. In those cases, you can add the URL to the LinkedIn company page as well as their website.

Here are some ideas to include in this section:

- **Public projects,** meaning where the final project can be seen by the public or in a public sphere. For example, a costume designer would include the shows for which they designed costumes, and an architect would include photos of buildings they designed. These projects can often also be featured in a portfolio, the link for which you can put in your Header and Featured sections.

- **Digital public projects,** meaning where the final project can be seen by the public online. This includes websites, videos, branding updates, and similar.

- **New line of businesses** for clients. If you have a client who successfully built a new line of business and you played a role in it, include it.

- **Advisory positions.** Advisory positions are unique in their scope and relationship. You can add them to your Experience section, but you could end up with a lot of "experiences" listed. I saw one profile that listed 16 different companies, which is a lot. Listing that many entries in the Experience section takes away from your core offering. Simplicity is key, which is why I like advisory positions in the Projects section.

- **Client projects.** Word these so you don't violate any NDA or trade secrets. For example, a fractional COO increasing efficiency by 50% by revamping logistics and procurement, or a sales coach sharing how their client increased sales by 200% by focusing on messaging and finding new ways to lead gen. Be as specific as possible, but note that this is NOT meant to replace experience entries.

- **Pitch or case competitions.** This can also be found under Honors and Awards, but here you can include your pitch deck and award certificate.

- **Work projects** for previous employers.

- **Podcasts or other AV projects** that you worked on.

The key here is to focus on successful projects that highlight your expertise, as well as projects that demonstrate the skills you want to use. The Projects section is meant to complement the Experience section, not replace it.

WHAT TO AVOID IN PROJECTS SECTION

Just because you can add them and what you did was real and hard and successful, doesn't mean it should be included. If you stick to the rules of relevance and success, then you may not need to worry about this. However, as a gentle reminder, here are things to avoid adding to your Projections section.

- **Anything that violates any agreements.** These could put you in legal jeopardy, or that could be seen as violating your client's trust or intellectual property. Depending on the type of work you do, you may want to get a release that allows you to mention the project without offering all the details.

- **Irrelevant projects.** This is especially if they showcase something you did that does not align with what you currently do, unless it's super awesome and you're really proud of it. For example, if you were on the team that designed the NASA Rover's arm function, and now you're teaching horse ballet (I promise you, horse ballet is a real thing), the dramatic difference is weird enough that it becomes a pretty cool talking point.

- **Projects you don't want to be associated with.** It doesn't matter how impressive or successful the project might be, skip it if you don't want to be associated with it for any reason. This is especially true if you have other projects that may be more relevant and where you can feature your experience, or because you don't want to do that type of work anymore.

- **Projects that failed.** I'm not talking about projects that are no longer in use because they are outdated, but ones that failed. An exception to that might be if you did great work but the client didn't use it right or didn't implement it or ran out of money. All of those are out of your control, so the question is whether you can talk about your project without throwing the client under the bus. The answer is often no, but keep them in mind.

If in doubt, add these to your LinkedIn ESD (emotional support document) so you can access the information later if the need comes up.

HOW TO FORMAT PROJECTS SECTION ENTRIES

The Projects section is specifically designed to showcase your work, whether your work is a major project you accomplished or part of a team. Plus, the way that projects is designed, you can add your skills, add a website or media, set a timeframe when it was completed, and provide the context, meaning you can link it to an entry you listed under experience or education.

For some founders and business owners, most of the projects you've done will be for clients or even when you were employed. For career professionals and job seekers, the projects were likely for your employer or even as a freelancer.

In both cases, as long as they highlight your skills and success, include them.

- **Title.** The title should be descriptive so that it interests the reader. "Bridge repair" doesn't have quite the same ring as "I-95 GW Bridge Traffic Planning (near NYC)." If possible, keep to similar formatting on project names.

- **Description.** Describe the project and your role. You have 2000 characters, but you don't need to list every detail. Oftentimes the goal of the project and what you did to contribute is enough. That's usually a few short sentences.

- **Skills.** List the skills you used working on this project. Be sure you use the same terms that you already have listed in the Skills section of your LinkedIn profile.

- **Media.** Use these to provide as complete a picture as possible for folks checking out your profile, without overwhelming them with irrelevant information. For example, adding a URL or a deck is reasonable. The costume designer could share photos of the costumes she personally designed for this event. Another idea is to add a link to a video of your client's testimonial. (Projects does not support video or GIFs, but you can create a playlist on YouTube or your website.)

  You can add several media to each project, including websites (URL), files, and photos.

- **Dates.** Dates provide context, especially if it's something that took a long time. However, this is not required information.

- **Add Contributor.** Real collaborations are awesome when they are handled well, especially if you have synergy. If you worked on a project with other folks on LinkedIn, this is a great time to share acknowledgment, especially if you work together regularly or you did a great job together. This could be with someone in the same firm (your business), but it doesn't have to be. Remember that adding people to this section does not diminish your contribution. It demonstrates that you have a great network that you can tap into. This is more beneficial than many realize.

- **Associated with.** Pick the experience or education where you worked on this project. If you worked on a cool project as an intern, this is where you would showcase that.

Projects are automatically sorted by dates, the most recent on top. If there is no date, then the entries resort to the order you entered them.

Finally, as you pick out projects to include here, remember that you do not need to have one project per client you've ever had, and you do not need to include any minimum number of projects.

AI/LLM PROMPT

There are so many things that can go in your Projects section, but one of the most common is case studies, so I've included that here. However, additional prompts can be found in the book bonuses.

Help me write a first-person LinkedIn Projects section entry that reads like a compelling case study.

> My goal for my LinkedIn profile is *[insert your goal, such as: get more clients / become a thought leader / find a job / sell my book].*

> I want the first two lines to:
> – Hook the reader with a bold result or intriguing challenge
> – Give context for what the project was

> Here are the details:
> Project name: *[insert short, descriptive project name]*
> Client or company (if shareable): *[insert name or "confidential"]*
> Timeframe: *[insert timeline or year]*
> Goal or challenge: *[brief description of the problem or desired outcome]*
> My role: *[what you were responsible for]*
> Approach taken: *[brief summary of what you did or how you solved it]*
> Result(s): *[insert specific outcomes, including metrics, transformations, milestones]*
> What this shows about me: *[insert skill, strength, or unique perspective]*

> Tone: Confident, clear, and strategic. *[edit to match your tone]*
> Keep it jargon-free and easy to scan.
> Highlight both *thinking* and *results*.

> What additional information do you need from me?

SAMPLE PROJECTS SECTIONS

To view examples, use QR code in Chapter 4 or at the end of this book.

ACTION PLAN

☐ Determine which of your skills you want to showcase.

☐ Determine what kind of projects you'd like to feature in the Projects section.

☐ Review your list of clients/employers and volunteering roles over the last 20 or so years.

☐ Brainstorm what you did for each of them and determine whether any of that could be considered projects.

☐ Cross off the projects that do not meet your strict criteria, that do not highlight the skills you want to share, or in most cases, were unsuccessful.

☐ Add projects that meet your criteria. Be sure to include graphics, websites, etc.

CHAPTER 17

Courses

THE PURPOSE OF THE COURSES SECTION is to showcase specific courses you took at the university level. It might be useful if you're recently out of college and need to demonstrate that you have knowledge in a particular field if you're looking for a job in that field.

The only exception might be if you are a college professor who wants to feature courses you teach and are offered at the school where you work. This provides context to your expertise, especially if you consult on the side. However, you'll want to make sure you note in the description that you teach the course.

This section is not usually useful for founders and other business owners.

CAREER PROFESSIONALS AND JOB SEEKERS

Everything in this section applies to you the same way it does founders and business owners, unless you are teaching at the university level (see above exception). Follow the guidelines below.

STRATEGY QUESTIONS

- Which courses have I recently taken that can be leveraged to demonstrate my subject area knowledge or expertise?

WHAT TO AVOID IN YOUR COURSES SECTION

Do not use this section to try to sell courses. It is not useful or appropriate for courses that you've created or are trying to sell. There is no place for live links or media. Instead, use the Featured or Services sections for those.

ACTION PLAN

☐ Skip this section, unless you teach at a college or university.

☐ If you teach at a college or university, add courses you teach that demonstrate your subject matter expertise, especially if you consult on the topic.

CHAPTER 18

Volunteering

THE VOLUNTEERING SECTION of your LinkedIn profile gives you an additional opportunity to highlight your skills and accomplishments, as well as allow others to learn what and where your interests outside of work are. It's also a great opportunity to showcase your values, and connect with someone over mutual interests or organizations.

In some ways, this section is similar to the Experience section, since you can highlight your skills and accomplishments. In fact, volunteer work is a great way to supplement your experience because you can learn new skills and showcase what you're able to do, even if you don't have enough experience.

CAREER PROFESSIONALS AND JOB SEEKERS

Everything in this section applies to you the same way it does founders and business owners. Follow the guidelines below, but keep in mind your potential employers rather than your ideal clients.

Note that some employers really like to see where their employees and prospects volunteer. If this is the case, be sure to only note what you don't mind they learn about you.

STRATEGY QUESTIONS

■ Which volunteer experiences do I have that complements or supplements my professional experience?

■ What kind of volunteer work can I do to supplement my professional experience, especially if I don't have a lot of experience in that area?

■ Which organizations have I already listed do not align with my current values or priorities? Which do?

WHAT TO INCLUDE IN YOUR VOLUNTEERING SECTION

Many of us do all sorts of volunteer/unpaid work. The key is discernment in what to include. Participating in a one-off golf outing fundraiser, for example, does not have the same gravitas as actually planning or chairing that fundraiser, unless it's an annual event and you personally raise a substantial amount of money each year, like through sponsorship or getting people to participate.

Most unpaid work can and should be included here. Some examples include:

■ Board positions for which you did not get paid, especially if it's not directly related to your industry. If you did not get paid for this role, you would add it here, although it can also be shared in your Experience section.

■ Sports coaching, especially for kids' sports.

■ Fundraising projects you headed up and about which you're particularly proud (and can demonstrate a number of skills).

■ Outreach projects that helped the organization with which you've worked.

■ Pro bono work for which you provided your services. This can be shared under projects, instead, depending on how many projects you have or if you have a portfolio.

■ Lectures offered at your local library.

You do not need to (nor should you) add every single volunteer work you've ever done. The key is to showcase your skills, your interests, and your values.

WHAT TO AVOID IN YOUR VOLUNTEERING SECTION

It's tempting to include every volunteering experience you've ever had in this section, but the adage "too much of a good thing" exists for a reason. Having 27 volunteering roles over 10 years is a bit much and sounds like you might be padding your resume, so to speak.

The Volunteering section is an opportunity to be strategic in highlighting the things that can bolster your LinkedIn profile.

Work that is best not included under volunteering:

- Anything you don't want to be publicly known.

- One-off volunteering that does not add to your profile.

- Organizations with whose ideals you don't agree.

- Volunteering where you left on poor terms.

- When none of your volunteering has a company page associated with them (all those dreaded gray squares), limit which ones you include.

- Old volunteering experiences (see below for parameters), especially one-off events.

- Volunteering experiences that are no longer relevant to you or that you don't want to be known for.

- Non-profits you founded, especially if you continue to manage it; that is better shared in experience or projects.

- Advising roles to companies or startups (often better shared in Projects section).

HOW TO FORMAT VOLUNTEERING SECTION ENTRIES

First, if the organization had an official job title for what you did, feel free to use that. Most of the time, however, they do not. In that case, use a descriptive job title.

This is not a resume, so do not offer a bulleted list of accomplishments. Instead, if the organization is not well known, write a sentence or two describing the work that it does. Then write another sentence or two describing the volunteering that you did.

Examples:

■ Planned annual easter egg hunt at local park for local neighborhood association. Coordinated volunteers and acquired donations.

■ Inaugural member of the school's parent-led, community-building organization. Headed up <list projects>.

■ Winners is a DC-based non-profit that aims to bring lacrosse to everyone who wants to play. Coached middle school boys each spring season, as well as during summer and holiday camps and special events.

■ Personally secured $350,000 in pledges for annual fundraiser supporting training programs for houseless parents.

TIMEFRAME

Volunteer work should be timely and relevant. Like the Experience section, you are unable to remove dates, so remove any old volunteer roles over 10 years old, unless you continue to volunteer there, or there is a compelling reason you want to keep it. This might be because you worked on a political campaign or one-time thing about which you're really proud or it allows people to know your values.

The reasons to remove old entries are the same as with experience: because you don't want your LinkedIn profile to age you, because you don't want to be publicly associated with that experience (for whatever reason, it's not always negative), or because it's not relevant.

However, if the most recent volunteering you've done is 15+ years ago, the best course of action often is to skip this section. Do not include it in your LinkedIn profile, because it's likely not relevant.

IF YOU DON'T HAVE ANY RELEVANT VOLUNTEER EXPERIENCE

Volunteering enough to warrant sharing the information on LinkedIn was, for the longest time, a uniquely American experience. In other words, not having volunteer experience isn't likely to be a deal breaker for anyone checking out your profile.

That said, if you do not have much experience in your field or focus area, volunteering with a local nonprofit does provide excellent experience and context, plus you can add the experience as an entry here.

AI/LLM PROMPT

Here is a sample AL/LLM prompt to craft a volunteering entry.

> Help me write a strong LinkedIn Volunteering section entry.
>
> My goal for my LinkedIn profile is *[insert your goal, such as: get more clients / become a thought leader / find a job / sell my book].*
>
> I want the first two lines to:
> – Explain what the organization does
> – Highlight the purpose or impact of my work
>
> Here are the details:
> Role/title: *[insert your role, e.g., Board Member, Volunteer Mentor]*
> Organization name: *[insert name]*
> Years involved: *[insert dates]*
> Mission of the org: *[brief description]*
> Why I got involved: *[personal reason or connection]*
> What I did: *[insert your responsibilities, leadership, programs led, etc.]*
> Impact/results: *[insert any measurable or notable outcomes]*
> Skills used or strengthened: *[insert relevant professional or personal skills]*
> What this shows about me: *[insert value, passion, or belief it reflects]*
>
> Tone: Warm, purposeful, and grounded, but not too formal. *[edit as necessary]*
>
> Write in first-person. Avoid clichés like "gave back." Focus on leadership, care, and connection.

SAMPLE VOLUNTEERING SECTION ENTRIES

To view examples, use QR code in Chapter 4 or at the end of this book.

ACTION PLAN

☐ Review existing Volunteering section entries.

☐ Remove any volunteering entries you don't want on your profile. If it helps or you may need the info later, transfer it to your LinkedIn emotional support document or folder.

☐ Add any new, relevant volunteer experiences. Check above for some ideas.

☐ If there's a dreaded gray box (no company page), check to see if that's changed and a company page was established since you added the entry. Sometimes you need to search on LinkedIn to find the proper name for it. Additionally, sometimes you need to create a new entry because the old one won't accept the new company page. Just copy and paste everything.

☐ Move advising and pro bono clients to your Projects section (when appropriate).

☐ Move non-profits you founded to Experience section, especially if you still run the organization or sit on its board.

☐ Add short descriptions and skills to the Volunteering entries you're keeping.

CHAPTER 19

Skills

THE PURPOSE OF THE SKILLS SECTION is to show off your expertise. However, how you use this section very much depends on your overall LinkedIn strategy. For founders and other business owners, this section isn't usually the most compelling section for your prospects. However, it's still worth doing right.

The good news is that LinkedIn now allows you to feature up to 100 skills, which is great when you're looking for a job. Now you can use specific terminology for similar or the same tasks that are noted in a job description. This is useful because companies and recruiters use sorting and AI-based tools that look for specific terms, so adding them to your profile simplifies this process.

The bad news is that LinkedIn now allows you to feature up to 100 skills. It's tempting as a founder or business owner to use the skills terms the same way as someone who is employed or looking for a job. Unless there is a compelling reason to do so (such as using your profile for dual-purpose, as described earlier in this book), do not highlight every variation of every skill you have. (See below for more details.)

CAREER PROFESSIONALS AND JOB SEEKERS

You will use this section differently than founders and business owners. Unlike founders and business owners, you may need to include more skills rather than fewer, depending on whether you're looking for a job. Business owners will be looking for the common denominator to limit the number of skills. You may need to add the different variations and/or details to capture the different language that different employers use. See below for more details.

STRATEGY QUESTIONS

- Which skills are my ideal clients looking for?
- What are the broadest but most relevant terms that best describe my skills?
- Where in my LinkedIn profile can I demonstrate I've used these skills?
- Career professionals and job seekers: Which skills are most relevant and important to highlight for potential employers and recruiters?

WHAT TO INCLUDE IN YOUR SKILLS SECTION

Your Skills section should only include the skills that your prospects want and that you use to accomplish the tasks your prospects need done. For most of us, this means limiting our Skills section to perhaps 12-15 skills, max. Exceptions will be if you have multiple businesses or if your profile is dual-purpose.

The key here is to not only include what you are good at, but also *what you want to do*. In my case, I know a lot about franchising, since I have experience as a franchisee, advising businesses to expand into franchising, and from the franchisor perspective. However, I hated my time in the franchise world and never, ever want to do it again. Therefore, I do not include anything franchise-related on my skills list.

Career professionals and job seekers should not only include what they want to do, but also what they are good at and what's required for their job. If you're in job-seeking mode, you may want to include skills that sound similar but that your prospective employers might use in a job description. Higher level jobs won't require this level of detail, but mid-level professionals might.

The best way to explain this might be an example. For example, if you are a marketing professional and one of your skills is video production, you don't need to break down video production into video, video production, video editing, video post-production, and more. The simple skill of "video" or "video production" is enough. Leadership is another example. You can choose leadership, team leadership, cross-functional team leadership, organizational leadership, strategic leadership, team building, and so many more. Or you can just use "leadership."

BONUS: When you ask for endorsements, it'll be easier for your colleagues to endorse you for the skills you want to highlight.

Conversely, if ALL you do is video production, it might make more sense to break it down into components, depending on how knowledgeable and experienced your ideal client is.

WHAT TO AVOID IN YOUR SKILLS SECTION

Do NOT include skills that are irrelevant to the actual execution for your services. For example, if you're a marketing expert or created and sell a non-alcoholic beverage, no one cares if you know how to use Word, Excel, or any Google Docs. In fact, I'd argue that this is a bare minimum if you own a business. However, if you're a VA or offer similar services, then these would be excellent skills to feature because people who are looking for VAs are often looking for these skills.

Career professions and job seekers, especially after entry level, should also skip these types of skills. If you don't understand how to use a basic word processor like Word or Google Docs, or using email, you need to brush up on these skills.

HOW YOU ENDED UP WITH SO MANY SKILLS LISTED

If you're like many folks, you probably didn't even realize how many skills you had listed in this section. Skills are added three ways: manually (you added the skills), when you add your experiences and assign skills that way, and if you took a LinkedIn skills training course. Any skill that you delete from the Skills section will also be deleted from the entry (experience, volunteering, projects) where you added them. Therefore, when you consolidate your skills, be sure to take note where a deleted skill is associated so that you can add that new skill to your entry.

WHY TO ONLY PICK A FEW SKILLS TO HIGHLIGHT

There are several reasons why you don't want to flood your Skills section with every skill you've ever had, reworded to match job descriptions, as one might do if they are looking for a job. For starters, if you're a founder or business owner, you're not looking for a job or trying to match a job description.

If you have too many skills listed, it's overwhelming to the reader and possibly to anyone who might be interested in endorsing you. Next, people who are not experts in your field will see redundancy, not detailed expertise. If I am hiring you to produce videos, I assume you'll understand the whole process from editing to final execution. Otherwise, why would I hire you? Finally, when you have too many skills listed, many will have no endorsements or very few. That's never a good look when you're hanging out your shingle as an expert in your field.

Career professionals and job seekers could also benefit from this advice. Too much is too much, period. The fewer skills that you list, the more likely you are to get your most important skills endorsed when you ask for endorsements.

ORGANIZE AND PRIORITIZE!

While you're trying to figure out which skills to keep and which to delete, it might be helpful to temporarily sort "like with like." To stick with our video production analogy, pick the skill that either best describes what you do in a general sense or the one with the most endorsements. If the numbers are all relatively low or the same, then pick the general one.

Next, organize them by the most important or relevant to the least. This way, the top skills will not only show up at the top of your list, but will also be the ones that are most likely to get more endorsements. Remember, when you look at someone's profile, the top two skills are shown on the front page of someone's profile.

Important: When you "edit" a skill, LinkedIn gives you the option to tell you where you used this skill. It will list experience, education, projects, volunteering, and publications. This gives you the opportunity to add a skill to boost credibility where you've done work.

ASK FOR ENDORSEMENTS

I know this seems obvious—and I know it's sometimes hard to do so—but ask your clients and colleagues for endorsements. Endorsements carry weight, especially if it's one of the first two skills that show up in your profile. Endorsing only takes a few moments to do, so that tends to be a very easy task for them. I've never heard of anyone getting mad at being asked; most likely, they'll ignore you. And that's okay.

SAMPLE SKILLS SECTIONS

To view examples, use QR code in Chapter 4 or at the end of this book.

ACTION PLAN

☐ Review your skills.

☐ Delete any skills not directly related to your offer/services (ex., Word, Excel, etc.).

☐ Delete any skills with zero endorsements unless you really, really want to be known as specializing in it.

☐ Combine skills and decide which overarching term best describes what you do. Unfortunately, endorsements you received for a term you delete do not get moved to another term, even if the meaning is very similar.

☐ Organize the terms so that the most relevant and popular are at the top.

☐ Edit each existing skill to make sure they are properly applied where you've used them.

☐ Ask clients and colleagues for endorsements.

CHAPTER 20

Recommendations

THE RECOMMENDATIONS SECTION of your LinkedIn profile is one of the most underutilized sections. Hiding all the way near the bottom, few realize how effective it can be.

Think of it like this: people like to read reviews before they buy or engage. We see ratings everywhere, from Yelp to Amazon to Google to Healthgrades. They are an effective tool and peer-rated (at least in theory). While LinkedIn recently started offering ratings in the Services section, recommendations are even more effective and they've been around a lot longer.

There are people who will check you out, then skip your About, Experience, Skills, Projects, etc., sections, and go straight to your Recommendations section. I've had people quote back to me what folks wrote about me years ago because they were impressed by what someone wrote. That recommendation closed the deal for me.

And yet, too many people do not ask for recommendations to their LinkedIn profile. We all should, every time we provide value to someone.

CAREER PROFESSIONALS AND JOB SEEKERS

Everything in this section applies to you the same way it does business owners. Follow guidelines below, but keep in mind your potential employers rather than your ideal clients.

STRATEGY QUESTIONS

■ On which topics could I use testimonials as proof-of-concept or expertise?

■ Who in my network is in a good position to offer a great testimonial? Are they a recent client/colleague/vendor and can they offer specific examples of my brilliance?

■ Are my current recommendations relevant and timely?

HOW LINKEDIN RECOMMENDATIONS WORK

You can give or request recommendations directly from your own LinkedIn profile. In fact, I recommend doing it this way because many people don't know how to use this feature. Additionally, you have a little more control over what you're requesting, providing context and parameters.

And here's the best part: You have to approve every recommendation before it is posted on LinkedIn. Therefore, if someone's recommendation sucks or says something that you don't want public, you can simply not approve it.

To give or request a recommendation:

1. It's helpful to ask someone ahead of time so they know to look for the request. They can proactively offer a recommendation as well.

2. Scroll down to the Recommendations section.

3. Click on the + sign and two options will appear: Ask for a recommendation and Give recommendation.

4. Next, find the person from whom you would like a recommendation. Hit Continue.

5. Fill out relationship and position at the time.

6. Personalized message can be skipped, but it's a great opportunity to provide context or whatever it is that you want them to say. You have 3000 characters, so if you wanted, you could even write it for them.

7. Let your contact know that you sent them a request.

WHO TO ASK

You have the option to ask clients, colleagues, and others who are in a position to know you and your work. In most cases, clients and colleagues are best because they can speak to your brilliance, work ethic, and outcomes.

Note that these relationships are not required to have some kind of financial arrangement. In my early days on LinkedIn, I'd get on networking calls and inevitably give advice that people found very helpful. Sometimes they would provide a recommendation as a thank you, because they were genuinely grateful. Today, if I really connect with someone and I've helped them out, regardless of the circumstances, I ask for a recommendation.

If you're just starting out or it's been a while since anyone has given you a recommendation, ask any of your previous clients, peers, colleagues, or supervisors to provide you a recommendation.

Don't get offended when more than half don't respond, even if you did an amazing job for them. People are busy and sometimes feel overwhelmed with being asked to provide a recommendation. This is why it's useful to give them some guidelines, preferably referring back to something they said to you.

You can say something like this: "Hi Sam, would you mind giving me a recommendation on LinkedIn? You told me that the efficiencies I put into place in your company allowed you to decrease your workload by 50% while doubling your revenue. I'd appreciate a recommendation that said this. A couple sentences would be perfect. Thanks!"

ASK FOR A RECOMMENDATION AT LEAST EVERY 6 MONTHS

I recently reviewed someone's profile, and the last time they received a recommendation was 11 years ago, during which time they seem to have changed careers at least twice. Considering how much has changed in those 11 years, those recommendations were not only dated, but also irrelevant.

Unless you work on projects that have a long life cycle or you have a more permanent, long-term arrangement (even if it's part-time), then you need more timely recommendations. If relevant, aim for at least one a quarter (every three months), and don't go longer than 6 or 12 months before you get another one. I've seen profiles where the last recommendation was from 2011. Really old recommendations that aren't reinforced with more recent ones have very low value and begs the question why there aren't more recent ones.

Note that when you ask for a recommendation, it is okay to ask them to specifically mention the thing for which you want to be known, or to not mention something else.

GIVING RECOMMENDATIONS

As a service provider and business owner, it is inevitable that you're in a position to receive more recommendations than give them. However, receiving recommendations without ever giving them is like being a selfish lover. You're getting all the attention, but not giving any. Not cool.

That said, recommendations cannot be quid pro quo; you cannot only give a recommendation if or when you get them. Instead, look for opportunities to give genuine recommendations. Some ideas:

▪ Clients or colleagues who are great to work with or you find brilliant in what they do.

▪ Someone whose webinar you attended and you learned something useful.

▪ A podcast host where you were a guest, especially if you had a good time.

▪ A thought leader who had a profound impact on you.

▪ A service provider who took good care of your client.

▪ An employee or subordinate who delivered great work or made your work life easier.

Basically, if you're in a position to compliment someone for the work they do, turn that into a public recommendation.

They do not have to be long. A couple sentences will often suffice.

ACTION PLAN

☐ Review existing recommendations to check for dates and relevance.

☐ Delete any that are problematic.

☐ Note on which topics you can use a testimonial.

☐ Brainstorm clients, colleagues, and others from whom you can ask for a recommendation.

☐ Ask for those recommendations and if possible, give guidelines (make it as easy as possible for them). Be sure to send an email or DM in addition to requesting it through the LinkedIn Recommendations section.

☐ Brainstorm folks for whom you can provide a recommendation.

☐ Send recommendations, and then DM or email them to let them know you did it, so they can look for it.

CHAPTER 21

Publications

EARNED MEDIA, OR MEDIA YOU DON'T PAY FOR, is recognized as the most credible form of media. If someone features your expertise in an article or publishes something you wrote, then that adds to your credibility as an expert in your field. This is especially true if you or your work is featured by a well-known and credible third party, such as *Fast Company*, *Forbes* or NPR.

The Publication section of your LinkedIn profile lets you show off where you've been published, whether in print, video, or audio. For scientists and medical professionals, these might include anything in peer-reviewed journals, for example. For others, this might be your podcast or if you were featured somewhere. The list of ideas is in the Action Plan below.

If you can provide a link, do it. Note that the link isn't required, but it does help. I do not recommend posting everything you've ever written, which I discuss below.

Additionally, the Publications section can be used to showcase where you've been featured and more (see below).

CAREER PROFESSIONALS AND JOB SEEKERS

Everything in this section applies to you the same way it does business owners. Follow guidelines below, but keep in mind your potential employers rather than your ideal clients.

STRATEGY QUESTIONS

■ Which articles have I written and were published by a well-known third party?

■ Which articles have I written that showcase my expertise?

■ Are there videos of my speaking engagements that showcase my expertise?

■ Do I have a podcast I'd like to show off?

■ Where have I been featured as a guest expert?

WHAT TO INCLUDE IN YOUR PUBLICATIONS SECTION

The Publications section serves a few purposes, the most important being that it allows you to demonstrate your expertise as a thought leader, and that a third party deemed you brilliant enough to publish your work, whether that's in print, in video, or in audio. Frankly, you could also include visual work, as well.

Less conventionally, the Publications section can also be used to feature articles, podcasts, or appearances where your expertise is featured. However, since this section automatically sets you up as the author (which you cannot remove), you will need to be clear in the description that you are *not* the author, but you're featured as a guest expert. This will help you avoid problems like claims of plagiarism.

The reason to include mediums that you did not author but where you're featured is because not everyone likes to write or gets published, but there are lots of people who are thought leaders and get featured as experts in someone else's article, podcast, and other content. While it's great to include these in the Featured section for a while, at some point you may want to clean up the Featured section for another purpose. In that case, you'll want to add them elsewhere on your profile.

Examples of what to include are listed in the Action Plan below.

Be sure to include the links for each of these articles and appearances. People will review them. Also, you'll be able to reference them when someone wants to see your work in action. It's so easy when your greatest hits are all in one place, and even better when that one place is on your LinkedIn profile. I've had people find and read/watch those links, which they then referenced when they set up a call with me.

Finally, I recently saw a coach add their lead magnets to their Publications section. I have mixed feelings about this. I personally think they are better placed in the Featured section or in a link-in-bio, but I can see the benefit. If you don't have much else to put in your Publications section, then this might work. However, if you do, then they could get lost in the rest of your publications. Use your own discernment.

WHAT TO AVOID IN YOUR PUBLICATIONS SECTION

Do not include every blog post you've ever written, either on your own website, LinkedIn's Pulse, or even a LinkedIn post. It's okay to include a popular post or a blog that showcases your expertise, especially early on when you're trying to build your own credibility, but this should not become a habit. The point is to show that others think you're a thought leader.

Anyone can post on LinkedIn or their own blog. Being published or quoted on a third-party website is considerably more effective and gives you credibility.

Do not include anything that does not put you in a positive light. While the old adage, "Any publicity is good publicity" may be true for large companies, that's not necessarily true for most of us. So unless there's a compelling reason to do so, stick to the stuff that makes you look good.

IF YOU DON'T HAVE PUBLICATIONS OR LINKS

If you don't have anything to put in this section, then leave this section off your LinkedIn profile. However, I strongly recommend that you find opportunities to show off your expertise so that you can add them to this section.

SAMPLE PUBLICATIONS SECTION ENTRIES

To view examples, use QR code in Chapter 4 or at the end of this book.

ACTION PLAN

The Publications section does not allow you to reorder your publication entries. Instead, it automatically lists them with the most recent date. For this reason, it's important to regularly update this section with new entries.

☐ Collect the links to publications or places where you can link the full article, video, or audio, including:
   ● Every article you've published, especially on third party publishers
   ● Posts that have gone viral on LinkedIn or elsewhere
   ● Every book(s) you've published
   ● Your podcast (where it's published)
   ● Any TEDTalks or other talks you gave
   ● Every article in which you've been featured
   ● Every podcast and appearance where you've been a guest

☐ Review these to determine which best showcase your expertise, thought leadership, values, or whatever you deem important.

☐ Delete existing publications that are irrelevant or not flattering, where the links are dead, or that do not best feature your expertise.

☐ Add your chosen publications to your Publications section. Add a short description that explains the gist of the article.

☐ For articles, podcasts, and appearances for which you are NOT an author, note this in the description.

☐ Find examples of how to do this in the book bonuses.

CHAPTER 22

Patents

IN CERTAIN INDUSTRIES, especially those based on science, medicine, technology, and engineering, patents are crucial to long-term success if they can be monetized. Owning patents is a flex that most of us will never experience. However, for those of us that do have patents, this section can show off your knowledge, expertise, and credentials in your field.

If you don't have any patents to your name or your company's name (a company that you own), then do not add this section.

CAREER PROFESSIONALS AND JOB SEEKERS

Everything in this section applies to you the same way that it does business owners.

STRATEGY QUESTION

- Which of my patents are relevant to the work I am doing now or can showcase what I'm capable of doing?

WHAT TO INCLUDE IN YOUR PATENTS SECTION

Owning a patent is an impressive accomplishment, but it's not always beneficial to share this information with the world at large. (See next section for those details.) To that end, include any well-known patents, any patents that you don't have to worry about triggering competition, and any patents pending.

Patents that you do not own but worked on (usually for an employer) should be featured in the Projects section.

WHAT TO AVOID IN YOUR PATENTS SECTION

Patents are meant to showcase your work, not work that belongs to someone else, whether that someone is a person or a company.

Therefore, do not include patents you do not own, expired patents (unless you note that it's expired but that it was originally yours), or patents that belong to the company for which you work. It's easy enough to look up patents, and being caught lying about one will never work out well.

BE JUDICIOUS AND STRATEGIC ABOUT WHAT YOU INCLUDE, ESPECIALLY IF YOUR IP IS NOT FULLY REGISTERED

Finally, if your patent is not yet registered in significant markets (US, Canada, China, parts of EU), you may want to talk to a patent attorney before you broadcast that you have IP that's been registered in a smaller country that doesn't have the leverage that larger economic powerhouses do.

ACTION PLAN

☐ Add patents that meet the criteria above.

CHAPTER 23

Honors & Awards

WHO DOESN'T LOVE ACCOLADES? Most people do, and sometimes, someone thinks you're so amazing, that they bestow awards or other honors on you. The Honors & Awards section is where you get to humble-brag about all of it.

Honors and awards are a form of social proof that amplifies your value to your industry or community. Leveraging them for your LinkedIn profile can demonstrate your knowledge, values, and more. They are high value because someone else has determined your worth. You didn't pay for it. You didn't create it for yourself. Instead, your peers or your community deemed you worthy. And that's pretty awesome.

CAREER PROFESSIONALS AND JOB SEEKERS

Everything in this section applies to you the same way it does business owners.

STRATEGY QUESTIONS

- What honors and awards have I received?
- Which of these will demonstrate my thought leadership, work success, or values?

WHAT TO INCLUDE IN YOUR HONORS & AWARDS SECTION

Ideally, you want to include honors and awards that reflect your most recent accomplishments and are relevant to your current profession, are judged by independent third parties, or are widely recognized as elite in some way.

Examples include:

- Honors or awards your team received for a project you worked on.
- Industry awards for which you were voted by your industry peers.
- Community service award for a passion project to which you donated your time and energy.
- Pitch competitions.
- Honorary degrees (can be listed here or under education).
- Bestseller designation on a prestigious list, like the New York Times Bestseller list.
- Grammy for music you wrote, or an Emmy for a show you produced, etc.
- Inc like Forbes' 50 Over 50, or 30Under30 lists.
- Awards and honors that demonstrate your credibility. For example, if you are an equine trainer today, then any awards you won for horse riding would be worth including.

I would also include well-known and extremely elite honors and awards you achieved, even if they aren't directly related to your business today, such as an Olympic medal. I had a friend who won the Tour de France the first year women were allowed to compete. I think that's super cool and would recommend that she include it on her LinkedIn profile, because it's not only an interesting talking point, but also an incredible achievement.

WHEN TO INCLUDE CHEEKY OR SILLY HONORS AND AWARDS

All this seriousness doesn't mean you can't be cheeky, either. Funny things make people laugh, and laughing people feel safe. If you can make someone laugh, you will be seen as relatable, and others will think that much better of you for making them laugh.

Add these honors and awards with an end goal in mind; strategy should always be top of mind! For example, if you're generally a serious scientist who managed to win an Ig Nobel Award, that would be worth including. It's funny, moderately irreverent, but also shows you have a sense of humor. (If you know, you know. If you don't, look it up.)

Another example is, depending on your brand and reputation, you could also include the "Best Worst Dad Jokes" award you got last year in your community's competition.

WHAT TO AVOID IN YOUR HONORS & AWARDS SECTION

The key to this section is being judicious and pragmatic about which of your accolades you include here. The "Best Smile" award you got as a silly award at work or the "Most Likely to Be Arrested" award you got in high school are not generally the kind of honors you should add to your LinkedIn profile.

Most awards and honors you received in college or graduate school 20+ years ago are rarely relevant today. But if you are a recent college graduate, then include that leadership award.

Academic designations like summa cum laude, valedictorian, etc., are usually best included with education, in the description of the associated degree.

ACTION PLAN

☐ Go through your records and find all the honors and awards you've received.

☐ Add the ones most appropriate. Be sure to include links to websites, videos, articles, or even a picture of the award.

CHAPTER 24

Test Scores

WE GET IT. You're a smarty pants who also does well on tests. However, I cannot think of many reasons to include test scores, but the Test Scores section for your LinkedIn profile exists, so clearly someone thinks it's important and relevant.

The purpose of Test Scores section is to show off your score on a highly competitive exam. For this reason, this section is probably best used by young folks who want to bolster their LinkedIn profile until they have better experience. However, I'm not really sure who cares about your SAT or ACT scores, especially since they are self-reported and cannot be independently verified.

That said, most founders and business owners will not need to use this section.

CAREER PROFESSIONALS AND JOB SEEKERS

This section is mostly geared towards you, so follow guidelines below.

STRATEGY QUESTIONS

- Do I have any test scores that might be worth adding to my profile?
- Am I in a profession that requires testing and high grades will improve my credibility?

WHEN TO USE THE TEST SCORES SECTION

There are a couple of situations where test scores might be useful in a professional setting. The first is proving language proficiency. To prove English proficiency, for example, people take TOEFL or IELTS. A higher score suggests higher proficiency, and if you're from a country where English is not your first language, this can be beneficial if you're looking for clients (or work) in an English-speaking country.

The second might be for professions that require rigorous testing, such as cybersecurity or professional licensing for engineering. You cannot add media here, so you cannot prove your credentials using this section, so I am not generally a fan of adding them here.

WHAT TO AVOID IN YOUR TEST SCORES SECTION

If you're already in college, past college, or never went to university, do not include your college entry exam scores, including SATs and ACTs.

Don't include exams that require only passing; there's no additional benefit or acknowledgment for higher scores.

Don't include scores for certifications that are listed in the Licenses & Certifications section.

ACTION PLAN

☐ Determine whether this section is worth including (for founders and business owners, as well as established career professionals, this is rarely the case).

☐ Include only scores that add to your credibility.

☐ If you do include this section, regularly check back and delete them when they are outdated or become irrelevant.

CHAPTER 25

Languages

AT THIS POINT, MANY OF US ARE MULTILINGUAL or know others who are multilingual. The purpose of the Languages section is to note which languages you know and at what level. It's super simple.

If you are not multilingual (meaning you only speak, read, or write one language, most commonly English), skip this section. No one will notice or think less of you.

CAREER PROFESSIONALS AND JOB SEEKERS

Everything in this section applies to you the same way it does business owners.

STRATEGY QUESTIONS

- Which languages do I have working knowledge of?
- Will any languages I know bolster my credentials or my LinkedIn profile?
- Are there any languages I don't want to include?

WHAT TO INCLUDE IN YOUR LANGUAGES SECTION

Only include languages for which you have a proficient or higher rate of fluency. Elementary-level fluency is underwhelming, so don't point that out. Once you hit proficiency, then add those languages.

WHAT TO AVOID IN YOUR LANGUAGES SECTION

Do not overstate your ability to communicate in any language. The world is small and it's easy to verify your proficiency, especially when we make video calls easily and frequently. All you need is to get on a call with someone who starts the conversation in the language you claimed proficiency. Bomb that and you lose all credibility. It's not worth it.

You are not required to add every (or even any) language you speak, so do not feel obligated to use this section.

ACTION PLAN

☐ Decide if you want to add other languages in which you are at least proficient.

☐ Add them to your profile.

CHAPTER 26

Organizations

IF YOU EVER WANTED AN OPPORTUNITY to boast about hanging out with the cool kids, the Organizations section was made for you.

The Organizations section benefits your profile in a few ways. First, it gives anyone who reads your profile an idea about your interests and values. If you belong to groups that champion female founders, others understand that you either identify as a female founder or support them. Second, it may help clarify how you see yourself by showing folks what kind of organizations you belong to. If you share what political party you belong to, that may influence how people see you and whether they want to do business with you. Third, it allows others in that group to find you for networking purposes or, if we're being honest, to sell to you due to your mutual interests and groups.

For all of these reasons, the Organizations section can be a powerful addition to the rest of your LinkedIn profile.

CAREER PROFESSIONALS AND JOB SEEKERS

In certain industries, belonging to certain organizations adds to your appeal and in some cases, is expected. You probably already belong to these organizations, so be sure to add them here.

Follow guidelines below, but keep in mind your potential employers rather than your ideal clients.

STRATEGY QUESTIONS

- Which organizations do I belong to?

- What kind of message do I want to send with the organizations I belong to? How will others see me, knowing I'm associated with that group?

- Do I need to supplement this section to find other organizations to which I should belong?

WHAT TO INCLUDE IN YOUR ORGANIZATIONS SECTION

This section is a great opportunity to share all the organizations of which you are a member, were a member, or that you support. The only required piece of information is the name of the organization.

However, you can also include your position (member, supporter, founder, etc.), which of your experience entries or education this is associated with, the dates, and the description.

As you consider which groups you'd like to add here, I suggest considering them from an outsider's perspective. If you belonged to a group where the head had a falling out with the community, do you want to be associated with that person? If you worked on a political campaign and someone decides that they won't do business with you because of it, are you okay with that?

Whatever you do, it's best to consider how others will perceive you as a result of seeing your connection in a particular organization.

Here are some ideas of organizations that you can include in this section:

- **Professional organizations.** Many professions, from medical specialties to engineering to life coaching, have professional organizations. Belonging to this type of organization often signals that you are serious about what you do.

- **Sororities and fraternities.** While most folks pledge during undergraduate, these are connections and associations that often last a lifetime.

- **Networking organizations.** In the US, this might include BNI or NeXco, which are membership-based networking organizations.

- **Communities,** especially if they are larger and/or well-known. They could be paid or free as long as they are active and can show what they do.

- **Local organizations or non-profits.** These might be good to list if they clearly demonstrate values that you want to showcase, but only if they add to your profile.

Note that organizations are listed first by dates and, barring dates, by the order that you entered them into this section.

Also, if you don't have many organizations to list, or it's been a very long time since you belonged to an organization, it's completely acceptable to skip this section. It's unlikely that someone won't do business with you because you don't have organizations listed.

WHAT TO AVOID IN YOUR ORGANIZATIONS SECTION

There's not much I wouldn't include as long as it reflects who you are today and what you do.

Do not add paid coaching programs you belong to, particularly if it's a small group. The exception is if there is a strong networking component or sense of community or identity, then it could make sense to add the organization.

Do not add organizations that are already listed under your experience section, or that you no longer align with for whatever reason. For example, if you worked for AARP in marketing, but are not a member, do not add it to your Organizations section.

In many cases, it does not make sense to add organizations that are already listed under your Volunteering section. For example, I founded a 501(c)(3) for my kids' school and sat on the board for years. I would not include that in my Organizations section because that organization does not reflect my professional goals or my current goals. However, I include it in my Volunteering section because of the work I did there. However, if your passion, profession, and causes all align (example, animal welfare), it could make sense to add aligned organizations here.

ACTION PLAN

☐ Decide how you want the Organizations section to reflect on you.

☐ Brainstorm all the organizations to which you've belonged over the years. Focus primarily on professional and work-related organizations.

☐ Cull through and determine which organizations deserve to be part of your LinkedIn profile. Consider how a viewer will judge you based on your association with each organization.

☐ Add organizations. LinkedIn does not allow you to reorder these entries, so they will need to get added in order of oldest to newest, or make sure you add the dates.

CHAPTER 27

Causes

THE VALUE OF THE CAUSES SECTION isn't readily obvious for founders and other business owners. The Causes section is a good way to share your interests and values, but that is also easily done through your Volunteering section. Causes seem to be more important for job seekers, though, because potential employers like to understand your values and interests to determine if you align with theirs.

Still, if you have causes that are near and dear to your heart, especially if they are not as obvious on your profile, you can absolutely use this section. For example, perhaps most of your Volunteering section examples were related to your kids' schools, but you also feel passionately about the environment. The Causes section is an opportunity to add environmentalism to your profile.

That said, I have never had anyone comment about the Causes section or even mention it in any context, so for most of us—especially founders and business owners—this section is okay to skip.

CAREER PROFESSIONALS AND JOBSEEKERS

Some companies have strong values, which will undoubtedly be reflected in their mission statement or somewhere on their website. If you share similar values, which are demonstrated by your causes and volunteer work, this can only help you. If your interests are diametrically opposed, it's probably best to leave this section off your profile.

STRATEGY QUESTIONS

■ What values or causes do I have that are not obvious on my LinkedIn profile?

■ Which ones are important enough that I want others to know that they are important to me?

ACTION PLAN

☐ Identify the causes/issues that are important to you.

☐ Determine where that might be obvious on your LinkedIn profile. This could be through Experience, Volunteering, Projects, or even in your About section.

☐ If none of these areas demonstrate your causes as an area of focus for you, and you want these to be known, then add them to the Causes section.

☐ Or skip this section. It's pretty low value.

CHAPTER 28

Company Page

THE COMPANY PAGE allows companies and organizations an opportunity to have a presence on LinkedIn without being tied to a specific personal profile, although it must be created by someone with a profile on LinkedIn.

It legitimizes the organization, allowing users to identify the organization as an employer or client. When there's a company page, someone reviewing your profile can click on the name of the organization or the favicon, and get brought right to the company page.

Additionally, it gives the organization another branding opportunity and allows fans and industry peers to "follow" the organization, keeping up with announcements by and news related to the organization.

If you own a company or work for yourself in any capacity, including freelancer, consultant, etc., then you need to set up a company page. If nothing else, it legitimizes your experience entry on LinkedIn profile. However, it also allows you another opportunity to connect with your audience, especially if they aren't people with whom you're connected on LinkedIn.

CAREER PROFESSIONALS AND JOB SEEKERS

This section does not apply to you unless you previously or currently own(ed) a business.

STRATEGY QUESTIONS

■ What do buyers need to know to do business with me or my business?

■ What is my sales pitch?

■ What are my ideal clients' most pressing concerns? What problem do they need solved?

WHAT TO INCLUDE ON YOUR COMPANY PAGE

Setting up a company page is pretty easy, but there are some elements that you want to make sure are included. You can find this under the Edit Page in the menu on the left.

■ **Banner.** This shows up behind the favicon, at the top of the page. You can use the same branding colors that you did on your personal profile, but the message should focus on the company, not you, unless you are promoting a specific offering for a limited amount of time.

Additionally, the size of this banner is different than on a personal page.

■ **Header > Page Info > Favicon.** This is the square box that shows up on your personal profile.

■ **Header > Page Info > Name.** The name of your company or organization.

■ **Header > Page Info > LinkedIn public URL.** You can change this, like you do for your personal page. If possible, I recommend using a URL that matches your other social media handles. It'll make it easier for you to remember.

■ **Header > Page Info > Tagline.** Think of this as your headline for your business. Make sure your tagline makes sense without context. A clever tagline that requires someone to know about you is not a great tagline, at least for LinkedIn.

■ **Header > Buttons.** You can add links to your calendar, portfolio, featured product/service, or your website. There is only one other opportunity for live links on a company page.

- **Home > Featured.** You can add up to three posts to the Featured section. This is a great place to add a post that includes a link to your website or a carousel about your products and services.

  NOTE: You have to make a post from your company page before using this feature.

- **About > Details > Overview.** Explain what your business does here. You have 2000 characters, but try to keep the description as short as possible. Mention your general offers and your ideal client. Use bullet points, since you cannot add graphics.

- **About > Details > Website URL.** Add your website URL here. If you don't have one, click the box below this.

- **About > Details > (required misc.)** You are required to fill in Industry, company size, company type. Skip phone number, unless it's to a physical address and not your cell phone.

- **About > Details > Specialties.** You can add up to 20, but like the Services section, you can't rearrange them after you've added them. You can make up your own, though.

- **About > Details > Locations.** You are not required to add a location, however if you do, use a metro area, not your hometown, unless this is a bricks-and-mortar location.

WHAT TO AVOID ON YOUR COMPANY PAGE

While your company page is another opportunity to share what you do, it is still not the place to share *everything* you do. So keep it short and sweet.

At the same time, be clear about what your company does. "ACME Inc. Making the world a better place" means nothing. As I've said many times throughout this book, don't make your audience think too hard to figure out what you do.

WHEN TO USE A SHOWCASE PAGE

A showcase page is set up exactly like a company page, but it is housed under your company and shows up in the right column under "Affiliated pages."

The downside to this is that you cannot add the showcase page to your experience or projects directly, but you can create a graphic that you link to it. You can use this graphic anywhere you want to share a website, like under featured, experience, projects, etc.

The upside is this gives you an opportunity to showcase projects that you want to feature or that are not directly related to your company's mission. For example, when I started talking about LinkedIn profiles and taught the masterclass that inspired this book, I created a showcase page, which I eventually turned into a company page since it's morphed into its own brand.

In fact, you should go and like it right now: **linkedin.com/company/lylip** or look up "Love Your LinkedIn Profile."

The option to turn a showcase page into a company page requires asking LinkedIn to do this. I found the process to be very fast (within a couple days).

INVITE CONNECTIONS TO FOLLOW YOUR PAGE

LinkedIn initially gives you 100 invitations each month (up to 250 as your connections count grows) so you can invite people in your network to follow your business page.

Actually, it's more accurate to say that you can have up to 100 or 250 invitations out each month. If you send out 100 or 250 invitations this month, and 12 connections accept the invitation and follow your page, you can then use those open invitations and send them to another 12 connections.

This is why it's so important to send out those invitations early in the month. Plus if you send them out too close to the end of the month, LinkedIn may count them toward next month's quota, as I've found out the hard way.

You'll find this on your dashboard at the top under Today's actions, or toward the bottom of the left column, where it says "Invite to follow." (Where to find this seems to move around, so you may need to Google the latest path to find that option.)

ACTION PLAN

☐ Create banner with branding color and message.

☐ Create square favicon with complimentary branding color. Keep words limited since this is small.

☐ Fill out sections above.

☐ Add a couple posts, at least one of which provides more information on products and offers. This one will be featured.

☐ Follow at least a couple other pages in your industry.

☐ Invite the maximum number of connections to like your page.

CHAPTER 29

Profile Cheat Sheet

THIS CHAPTER OUTLINES WHICH TYPES OF PROFILES could benefit from which sections. The guidelines below are meant to be just that: guidelines. The goal is to give you a jumpstart to planning out your profile.

If a section is not relevant to you despite the fact your goal matches one of the ones listed below, then skip that section.

Notes:

- Sections that are obvious or require unique entries are not listed. Most people don't own patents, for example, and you're the only one who can determine whether your licenses and certifications should be listed.

- Where appropriate, quick notes are added.

- Be sure to visit the corresponding chapter to learn what's best included and how to format each section for best results.

ALL PROFILES

Some sections are not optional, and others should not be considered optional.

These include:

- Banner

- Profile headshot

- Headline

- Intro section (see that chapter to see which parts to skip)

- About
- Featured
- Experience
- Skills
- Recommendations

SERVICE PROVIDERS

Service providers provide services to clients. They own their own business, own an agency, or even be a freelancer or solopreneur. Their audience tends to be prospects (potential clients) as well as current clients. They essentially fall into two categories:

1. **Thinkers and planners,** such as consultants, fractional CXOs, strategists, coaches, and course creators.

2. **Doers,** such as freelancers, web designers and developers, marketing specialists, social media managers, DFY (done for you) services, and DWY (done with you) services.

There is a lot of overlap between these two categories, so the notes below are relevant to your primary goal for your profile. If there are no notes in the section listed, the corresponding chapter provides what you need to know.

Section	Thinkers/planners	Doers
Banner	Transformation you provide or specific services	Benefit you provide or specific services
Headline	Title, something that can identify market, something that makes you interesting and memorable	What you do, who for (without using help statement), why someone should hire you
About	Origin story, methodology if relevant, what people say about your work	What your clients can expect from you, how you make clients' lives easier
Services	See chapter	See chapter
Featured	Calendar link, lead magnet, link to methodology or website, latest brag (where you've been featured), thought leadership, newsletter sign-up	Portfolio, testimonials, link to website
Experience	Use company page	Use company page (yes, even freelancers!)
Projects	See chapter	See chapter
Skills	See chapter	Focus on what your clients want
Publications	See chapter	See chapter

FOUNDERS AND ENTREPRENEURS

These are the folks who start businesses that do not fall into the Service Providers category above. Their businesses are product-based, either physical products or digital products. They often have big visions and may be looking for money to fund their startup and growth, although many are not. They are often passionate about their business, solving problems that many people don't even realize need solving. Their audience includes their industry peers, advisors, members of their ecosystem (such as the startup ecosystem), potential funders (if relevant), and clients and potential clients. Their audience is looking for an investment or a problem to be solved.

Section	Founders and Entrepreneurs
Banner	The problem their product solves
Headline	Founder, passion about problem being solved, status
About	Your and/or your company's origin story, can also mention your company is prospecting for funding (do not ask for funds here)
Featured	Website, general pitch (not specific pitch deck), calendar (if relevant), posts that share where you've won awards and grants for business idea
Experience	Company page is accurate, any experience that reinforces your experience in your industry or relevant skills
Projects	Anything that will reinforce your experience in that industry or passion about your product/industry
Publications	See chapter

THOUGHT LEADERSHIP

Thought leaders are the ideas people. They are the speakers, authors, podcasters, and often content creators, like influencers. They are known for what they do, their philosophy or approach, and what they are setting out to accomplish. Their audiences trust them and like to hear what they have to say.

Section	Thought Leadership
Banner	Philosophy, approach, or what you're known for
Headline	Name of movement you've founded or what you're trying to accomplish, where people can find your work
About	Your origin story and that you're open to offers to show up
Featured	Portfolio of latest appearances, One Sheet, link to purchase books you've written
Experience	List business thought leadership, use company page for details, list how to reach you, include One Sheet and any relevant info
Skills	Focus on areas of expertise featured in your thought leadership
Publications	See chapter

CAREER PROFESSIONALS AND JOB SEEKERS

Career professionals and job seekers work for someone else. They do not own the company for which they work. Their goal may be to have a presence on LinkedIn to add to their credibility or, as in the case of job seekers, to supplement their CV or network for job prospects. Their audience is often made up of personal connections and industry peers, or in the case of job seekers, connections in companies they'd like to work for.

Section	Career professionals	Job seekers
Banner	Your philosophy or approach that makes you really good at what you do; can also include high-level skills	Type of job you seek + what makes you good at it (why someone should hire you)
Headline	Title, quality skill, something that makes you interesting and memorable	Quality skill, something that makes you interesting and memorable, that you're looking for a job (use creative wording)
About	Summary of professional experience (just a few sentences). If you're planning to consult, your origin story will also work	Summary of professional experience, type of place you're looking to work for, why they should hire you (all in only a few sentences)
Featured	Latest brag (where you've been featured), latest accolades, post about what is going on with your employer if you're on that team	Portfolio (if relevant), website (if relevant), accolades for which you've received recognition
Experience	Make sure to use employer's company page	Make sure to use company page for previous employers
Projects	See chapter	See chapter
Skills	See chapter	See chapter
Publications	See chapter	See chapter

CHAPTER 30

What Goes Where Index

BELOW IS AN EXTENSIVE LIST OF THINGS that can be included in a LinkedIn profile. While it doesn't include every possible scenario, this should give you an idea where things can be placed within your profile. These are *OPTIONS*. For items that have multiple places to go, you don't need to, nor should you, include the item in every location mentioned. Pick the one(s) that suits you best (because yes, you can include an item in multiple places).

Notes:

- Unless noted otherwise, these items are about you, not your clients, company, or anything else.

- When Experience, Volunteering and other sections are mentioned, the items listed refer to a specific entry, not every entry collectively within that section

Accolades. *honors & awards*

Address. *do not include, except if you have a physical location*

Advisory positions. *projects, experience*

Articles, co-authored. *publications*

Articles, written. *publications*

Articles, you're featured. *publications, with attribution to author*

Awards. *honors & awards*

Birthday. *do not include*

Blog. *do not include*

Blog link. *publications, featured, intro*

Board positions. *volunteering*

Books in which you're featured. *publications*

Books to which you've contributed. *publications*

Books you've published. *featured, publications*

Book you're launching. *banner, featured*

Branding, where to use. *banner, services, featured, experience, company page, projects*

Business details, yours. *company page, services, featured*

Business summary. *experience, services*

Calendar link. *website in intro, featured*

Case studies. *projects*

Certifications, expired. d*o not include*

Certifications. *licenses & certifications*

Coaching certification. *licenses & certifications*

Coaching program, you joined. *do not include*

Coaching program, yours. *featured, services, experience, maybe about (but only overview)*

College. *education*

College activities. *do not include*

Community, you belong. *organizations*

Community, yours. *featured, services, experience, maybe about*

Courses you offer. *featured, experience graphics, services graphics*

Courses you teach (college-level). *do not include, courses*

Courses you've taken. *do not include, or courses*

Course you're launching. *banner, featured*

CV, available in full. *do not include, maybe featured*

CV, details. *do not include*

CV, highlights. *experience*

Degrees. *education*

Email address. *do not include*

Employer's details. *company page (probably not yours)*

Employment type. *do not include if founder/business owner*

Freelance work. *company page (yours), experience (under one entry)*

Funding info deck. *do not include, or featured, experience*

Funding request (looking for funding). *about, banner, headline, maybe projects*

Graduate school. *education*

High school. *do not include*

Honors. *honors & awards*

Ideal client profile. *services, about, experience, featured, maybe headline*

Keynote speeches you offer. *featured, on one sheet*

Languages. *languages*

Lead magnet. *featured, experience, maybe publications*

Licenses. *licenses & certifications*

Link-in-bio, like Link.tree or similar. *website in intro, featured, experience*

Looking for clients. *See* Ideal client profile

Looking for job. *headshot, about, maybe banner*

Masterclasses you teach/offer. *featured, experiences graphics, services graphics*

Memberships. *organizations, maybe headline, maybe about*

Mentions. *publications, or temporarily featured post*

Methodology, yours. *featured, services graphics, company page, or do not include*

MVP (startups). *featured, experience*

Newsletter. *publications, featured, website in intro*

Offer deck. *services, featured, experience*

Offers. *services,*

One Sheet. *featured, website in intro, experience*

Origin story, your business. *about, company page*

Origin story, yours. *about, or do not include*

Patents. *patents*

Philosophy, yours. *banner, about*

Phone number. *do not include*

Pitch. *featured*

Pitch deck. *do not include (usually)*

Podcast, guest appearance. *publications with attribution to host*

Podcast, yours. *featured, publications, experience*

Portfolio. *intro, featured, services, company page, experience*

Prices. *services, or do not include*

Problems you solve. *banner, headline, about*

Pro bono work in your industry. *volunteering, projects, maybe experience*

Products. *banner, experience, about, maybe projects*

Projects. *projects*

Recommendations. *recommendations*

Resume. *See* CV

Secondary school. *See* High school

Showcases. *projects*

Skills. *skills*

Social media links. *experiences under relevant company, featured section with link-in-bio, website in intro section*

Speaking gigs, announcements. *featured (temporarily), banner (temporarily)*

Speaking gigs, recorded. *publications*

Speeches. *featured, on one sheet*

Success stories. *projects*

Testimonials, video. *featured*

Testimonials, written. *recommendations*

Test scores. *do not include (see test course section)*

Trade school. *education*

Transformation, your clients. *banner, about, services*

Unique selling proposition. *about, company page*

University. *education*

Volunteering. *volunteering, projects*

Website. *website in intro, featured, company page, experience*

Weird but interesting. *headline, maybe about*

Zip code. *use closest metropolitan area*

APPENDIX

Bonus Content

The following bonus content can be found on the companion website:

- Layout of a LinkedIn profile (wireframe)
- Examples of many sections (even if example is not explicitly noted as available)
- Additional and updated AI/LLM prompts
- Bonus videos
- Link to YouTube channel and other socials
- Explainer articles and videos (or links to them)
- And so much more!

https://loveyourlinkedinprofile.com/secret-book-bonuses

About the Author

NATALIE BERTHE IS A STARTUP AND GROWTH STRATEGIST who turns messy, complex business problems into clear, actionable solutions. A serial founder of more than a dozen ventures—both businesses and nonprofits—she helps entrepreneurs build businesses from purpose to profit without gatekeeping, jargon, or performative nonsense.

Her clients have transformed ideas sketched on napkins into apps, consultancies, products, and movements that make an impact. Natalie cuts through the noise, asks the questions others overlook, and creates momentum that delivers real results. She makes strategy accessible, energizing, and actionable.

She's published in *Fast Company* and *Startups,* regularly featured in podcasts and media outlets, and holds both an MBA and an MA in International Communication. Readers and clients value her honesty, sharp thinking, and ability to turn strategy into clarity and results.

At the core of Natalie's work is a simple belief: business can be both purposeful and profitable, and clarity is what makes it happen.

www.ingramcontent.com/pod-product-compliance
Lightning Source LLC
Chambersburg PA
CBHW040855210326
41597CB00029B/4856